Ruby on Rails in Action

Building Dynamic Web Applications Leverage Rails to build robust and maintainable web apps

THOMPSON CARTER

Table of Content

TABLE OF CONTENTS

Introduction

MASTERING RAILS DEVELOPMENT

Welcome to **Mastering Rails Development: Building Scalable and Robust Web Applications with Ruby on Rails**! Whether you are an experienced developer or just starting with Ruby on Rails, this book provides a comprehensive guide to mastering one of the most powerful and developer-friendly web frameworks available. Rails is known for its simplicity, productivity, and robust community, making it an excellent choice for building modern web applications. This book will walk you through the entire Rails development process—from the foundational concepts to advanced techniques, guiding you toward building scalable, maintainable, and efficient applications.

What is Ruby on Rails?

Ruby on Rails, or simply Rails, is a **full-stack web framework** written in **Ruby** that emphasizes convention over configuration (CoC) and don't repeat yourself (DRY) principles. These philosophies make it easy to develop applications quickly without needing to make redundant decisions or write boilerplate code. Rails provides a rich ecosystem, including tools for handling database migrations, routing, views, and security, among other essentials required in modern web development.

Rails is designed for developers who want to focus on solving business problems, not on repetitive or low-level technical details. It's ideal for building applications with a **relational database**, **API-first** structures, or modern **single-page applications (SPAs)**.

Who is This Book For?

This book is written for **Rails developers at all skill levels**. Whether you're just getting started with Rails or are already an experienced developer looking to deepen your understanding, this book will help you:

- Learn the foundational principles of Rails, including its **MVC architecture**.
- Master the full Rails development cycle, from setting up a project to deploying it in a production environment.
- Understand best practices for writing clean, maintainable code that's easy to scale.

- Explore real-world examples of implementing advanced features like **authentication, API integrations, real-time communication**, and **task management** systems.

While the book provides in-depth explanations and step-by-step examples, it also includes advanced topics for experienced developers, ensuring it remains relevant as your skills grow and evolve.

What You Will Learn

This book is divided into clear, concise sections to help you gradually build your knowledge of Rails development. You will learn how to:

- **Set up and configure Rails** for different environments, including using the **Rails console**, managing dependencies, and configuring databases.
- **Understand Rails architecture** through its **Model-View-Controller (MVC)** structure, gaining a solid grasp of how Rails works under the hood.
- **Implement common features** like **user authentication, CRUD operations**, and **data validations** efficiently with minimal code.
- **Integrate third-party services** and **APIs**, enabling your app to connect to external systems.

- Use tools like **RSpec** and **Capybara** for **testing and debugging**, ensuring that your applications are robust and bug-free.
- **Deploy your Rails application** to cloud platforms like **Heroku**, **AWS**, and **DigitalOcean**, automating workflows through **CI/CD pipelines**.
- **Monitor and log** your application in production to ensure its performance is optimal, using tools like **New Relic**, **Lograge**, and **Sentry**.
- **Scale your Rails application** to handle growing traffic and performance needs by implementing best practices and optimizing key components.

Building Real-World Applications

This book focuses on practical, real-world examples, teaching you how to build a **full-stack Rails application** from scratch. You'll work on a project-based approach to gain hands-on experience in each topic. By the end of the book, you'll have a fully functional web application that can be deployed to production and maintained for the long term.

From setting up the project, implementing authentication, integrating third-party APIs, managing databases, and deploying to production environments, this book covers all the steps needed to build a scalable and efficient web application with Rails.

Learning from the Experts

Throughout the book, we will also touch on **best practices** for code organization, maintainability, and scalability, ensuring your applications are well-structured and easily extensible. The concepts and patterns discussed in this book will not only apply to your current Rails projects but will also serve as a solid foundation for building any future web applications with Rails.

What to Expect from Each Chapter

Each chapter in this book focuses on a specific aspect of Rails development, starting with the basics and gradually moving to more complex topics:

- **Chapter 1: Introduction to Ruby on Rails** – Gain a comprehensive understanding of Rails and its role in web development.
- **Chapter 2: Setting Up Your Development Environment** – Learn how to configure your machine for Rails development, install essential tools, and set up a database.

- **Chapter 3: MVC Architecture in Rails** – Explore Rails' core design philosophy through the MVC pattern and how it shapes your applications.

- **Chapter 4: Building Your First Rails Application** – Create your first Rails app and gain hands-on experience with the Rails workflow.

- **Chapter 5: Authentication and Authorization** – Implement user authentication using **Devise** and learn how to manage user permissions.

- **Chapter 6: CRUD Operations** – Learn how to create, read, update, and delete records in the database efficiently.

- **Chapter 7: Integrating APIs and External Services** – Learn how to connect to third-party services, from social media APIs to weather data integrations.

- **Chapter 8: Testing and Debugging Rails Applications** – Use testing frameworks like **RSpec** and debugging tools like **byebug** to ensure your code is robust and error-free.

- **Chapter 9: Deploying and Maintaining Rails Applications** – Deploy your app to cloud services and automate deployment processes with **CI/CD**.

- **Chapter 10: Scaling Rails for High Traffic** – Learn how to optimize Rails apps to handle increasing traffic, from database indexing to caching strategies.

By the end of the book, you'll be equipped with the knowledge and experience needed to tackle even the most challenging Rails projects.

The Future of Ruby on Rails

As Rails continues to evolve, this book will keep you up to date with the latest Rails features and best practices. We will cover upcoming trends, such as **Hotwire** for seamless front-end integration, **WebSockets** for real-time applications, and the rise of **API-first** development in the modern web landscape.

Rails remains a powerful, adaptable framework for building modern web applications, and with the skills gained from this book, you'll be prepared to leverage Rails for building web applications that are both efficient and future-proof.

Conclusion

Whether you're building a simple blog or a complex, high-traffic web application, this book will guide you every step of the way. Rails' emphasis on productivity, simplicity, and convention makes it the perfect choice for developers who want to quickly build maintainable and scalable web applications. So, let's dive into the world of Rails, learn how to harness its power, and start building amazing applications that meet the needs of users today and tomorrow.

Happy coding, and welcome to **Mastering Rails Development**!

CHAPTER 1: WHY RUBY ON RAILS?

Introduction

Web development has evolved significantly over the years. From static HTML pages to dynamic, interactive web applications, the demand for efficient, maintainable, and scalable solutions has never been higher. In this chapter, we'll explore why **Ruby on Rails** (often referred to simply as **Rails**) has become a powerful choice for developers building modern web applications.

By the end of this chapter, you will:

- Understand **how web development has evolved** and why frameworks like Rails exist.
- Learn the **key advantages of Rails** over other web development frameworks.
- Explore **real-world applications** that leverage Rails for scalability and maintainability.

1.1 The Evolution of Web Development

The Early Days: Static HTML and CGI Scripts

Before frameworks like Ruby on Rails existed, websites were primarily built using **static HTML**, which meant every page was manually written and displayed as-is. If developers needed dynamic content (e.g., showing personalized information to users), they had to write **Common Gateway Interface (CGI) scripts** using languages like **Perl** or **PHP**.

This approach had several problems:

- **Scalability Issues**: Manually handling requests for dynamic content was inefficient.
- **Code Repetition**: Developers often had to rewrite the same logic multiple times.
- **Security Risks**: Lack of structured coding practices led to vulnerabilities.

The Rise of Web Frameworks

To solve these challenges, frameworks were introduced to **standardize development**, improve **code reusability**, and **enhance security**.

Popular web frameworks that emerged included:

- **PHP Laravel** – A structured framework for PHP.
- **Django** – A Python-based framework following the "batteries included" philosophy.

- **ASP.NET** – Microsoft's enterprise-grade web framework.
- **Ruby on Rails** – A highly productive framework known for its **convention over configuration** approach.

Why Did Ruby on Rails Stand Out?

Rails quickly gained popularity because:

1. It followed a **developer-friendly philosophy** that allowed for **rapid application development**.
2. It enforced best practices like **MVC architecture, Active Record ORM**, and **RESTful routing**.
3. It came with built-in tools for **database management, testing**, and **security**.

1.2 Advantages of Ruby on Rails Over Other Frameworks

1. Convention Over Configuration (CoC)

Rails follows the **CoC** principle, which means developers **don't have to configure everything manually**. Instead, Rails makes intelligent assumptions about how things should work, reducing the time spent on boilerplate code.

For example, in other frameworks, you might need to manually configure how models and database tables connect. In Rails, this happens automatically:

```ruby
class User < ApplicationRecord
  has_many :posts
end
```

- The `User` model automatically maps to a `users` table in the database.
- Rails understands **pluralization**, so `Post` would map to a `posts` table.
- This reduces unnecessary **configuration work**.

2. Rapid Development with Scaffolding

Rails allows developers to **generate entire application structures** with a single command. For example, if you need a basic blog application:

```sh
rails new blog_app
cd blog_app
rails generate scaffold Post title:string body:text
```

This automatically creates:

- A **database model** for Post
- A **controller** for handling HTTP requests
- Views for **displaying, editing, and creating** posts
- A **database migration** to create the necessary table

Compared to other frameworks where developers must set up each component manually, Rails **saves hours of work**.

3. Built-in Active Record ORM

Instead of writing raw SQL queries, Rails provides **Active Record**, an **Object-Relational Mapping (ORM) tool** that simplifies database interactions.

For example, retrieving all users in SQL:

```sql

SELECT * FROM users;
```

In Rails:

```ruby

User.all
```

This **abstracts database complexity** and makes querying more intuitive.

4. Strong Security Features

Rails comes with built-in security measures:

- **Protection against SQL Injection**
  - o Automatically sanitizes database queries.
- **Cross-Site Scripting (XSS) Protection**
  - o Escapes user input in views.
- **Cross-Site Request Forgery (CSRF) Protection**
  - o Ensures requests originate from legitimate users.

These features **reduce common security risks** without requiring additional setup.

5. Large Community & Ecosystem

Rails has a **huge developer community**, meaning:

- Thousands of **open-source gems (plugins)** are available for adding features.
- A wealth of **tutorials, guides, and forums** make problem-solving easier.
- Major companies use Rails, ensuring **long-term support and job opportunities**.

Some popular gems include:

- **Devise** – User authentication.
- **Pundit** – Authorization.
- **Sidekiq** – Background job processing.

1.3 Real-World Applications Powered by Rails

Many successful companies have **built and scaled their platforms** using Rails. Let's look at some examples.

1. Shopify

A leading **e-commerce platform** handling millions of merchants worldwide. Shopify chose Rails because of:

- **Rapid development capabilities** – Quick iteration and feature deployment.
- **Scalability** – Handles **millions of transactions daily**.
- **Security features** – Protects financial data and user transactions.

2. GitHub

One of the world's largest **code hosting platforms**.

- Uses Rails for **handling repositories, issues, and version control**.
- Implements Rails' **background jobs** to process millions of pull requests efficiently.

3. Airbnb

A **global vacation rental marketplace**.

- Uses Rails to handle **user accounts, bookings, and payments**.
- Leveraged **Rails' API capabilities** to integrate with third-party services.

4. Basecamp

The **project management tool** built by the same creators of Rails.

- Relies on Rails for its **simple yet powerful interface**.
- Demonstrates how Rails supports **clean, maintainable code**.

5. Fiverr

A **freelance marketplace** connecting buyers and sellers.

- Built with Rails for **fast, interactive user experiences**.

Ruby on Rails in Action

- Uses **caching and background jobs** for handling transactions.

These companies prove that **Rails is not just for small projects**—it powers some of the largest, most complex applications on the web.

Chapter Summary

In this chapter, we explored: **The history of web development** and the rise of frameworks like Rails. **Why Ruby on Rails stands out**, thanks to its **convention over configuration, rapid development tools, and strong security**. **Real-world examples** of successful applications built with Rails, proving its power and scalability.

In the next chapter, we'll **set up our development environment**, ensuring we have all the tools needed to build our first Rails application.

Next Chapter → Setting Up Your Development Environment

CHAPTER 2

SETTING UP YOUR DEVELOPMENT ENVIRONMENT

Introduction

Before we start building applications with Ruby on Rails, we need to set up a **proper development environment**. This ensures that everything runs smoothly, from writing code to managing dependencies and databases.

By the end of this chapter, you will: Install **Ruby** and **Rails** on your system. Understand **version managers** like **RVM** and **rbenv**. Set up **databases** and essential development tools.

2.1 Installing Ruby and Rails

Why Do We Need Ruby?

Rails is built using **Ruby**, so before we install Rails, we must install **Ruby** itself. Different operating systems require slightly different installation processes.

Installing Ruby on macOS

If you're using a Mac, you can install Ruby using **Homebrew**:

sh

```
brew install ruby
```

To verify the installation, run:

sh

```
ruby -v
```

This should output something like:

nginx

```
ruby 3.2.2
```

Installing Ruby on Linux (Ubuntu/Debian-based systems)

On Linux, use **apt** to install Ruby:

sh

```
sudo apt update
```

38

```sh
sudo apt install ruby-full
```

Then, check the version:

```sh
sh
```

```sh
ruby -v
```

Installing Ruby on Windows

For Windows users, the easiest way to install Ruby is through **RubyInstaller**.

1. Download the installer from rubyinstaller.org.
2. Run the installer and select the latest stable version.
3. Ensure that the option **"Add Ruby to PATH"** is checked.
4. Verify the installation by running:

```sh
sh
```

```sh
ruby -v
```

Installing Rails

Once Ruby is installed, installing Rails is straightforward using the **gem** package manager:

```sh
sh
```

```
gem install rails
```

After installation, check the Rails version:

```
sh
```

```
rails -v
```

Output:

```
nginx
```

```
Rails 7.0.4
```

Now that Rails is installed, we can move on to managing different Ruby versions.

2.2 Using Version Managers (RVM and rbenv)

Different Rails projects may require different versions of Ruby. To manage multiple Ruby versions easily, we use a **version manager**.

Option 1: RVM (Ruby Version Manager)

RVM allows you to switch between different Ruby versions effortlessly.

Installing RVM

Run the following command:

```sh
```

```sh
curl -sSL https://get.rvm.io | bash -s stable
```

Reload your terminal:

```sh
```

```sh
source ~/.rvm/scripts/rvm
```

Now, install the latest stable Ruby version:

```sh
```

```sh
rvm install 3.2.2
rvm use 3.2.2 --default
```

Check the version:

```sh
```

```sh
ruby -v
```

Switching Ruby Versions with RVM

If you need to use an older Ruby version:

sh

```
rvm install 2.7.6
rvm use 2.7.6
```

To list all installed Ruby versions:

sh

```
rvm list
```

Option 2: rbenv

Another popular version manager is **rbenv**. It's lightweight and does not override system settings.

Installing rbenv (macOS/Linux)

sh

```
git clone https://github.com/rbenv/rbenv.git
~/.rbenv
echo 'export PATH="$HOME/.rbenv/bin:$PATH"' >>
~/.bashrc
echo 'eval "$(rbenv init -)"' >> ~/.bashrc
```

```sh
source ~/.bashrc
```

On macOS, you can also install it using Homebrew:

```sh
brew install rbenv
```

Installing Ruby with rbenv

```sh
rbenv install 3.2.2
rbenv global 3.2.2
```

To verify:

```sh
ruby -v
```

Switching Ruby Versions with rbenv

To list all installed Ruby versions:

```sh
rbenv versions
```

To switch between versions:

```sh
```

```
rbenv global 2.7.6
```

☞ **Which One to Choose?**

- Use **RVM** if you want a feature-rich version manager with gemsets.
- Use **rbenv** if you prefer a lightweight, simple tool.

Both achieve the same goal, so choose the one that best fits your workflow.

2.3 Setting Up Databases and Essential Tools

Choosing a Database

Rails supports **multiple databases**, but the most commonly used ones are:

SQLite (default for small projects)

PostgreSQL (recommended for production)

MySQL (widely used for enterprise applications)

Installing SQLite (Default for Rails)

SQLite comes pre-installed with Rails, so no extra setup is needed.

To verify:

sh

```
sqlite3 --version
```

Installing PostgreSQL

PostgreSQL is a more powerful, scalable database. To install:

- **macOS**:

  sh

  ```
  brew install postgresql
  ```

- **Ubuntu/Debian**:

  sh

  ```
  sudo apt update
  sudo apt install postgresql postgresql-
  contrib
  ```

- **Windows**: Download from postgresql.org.

45

To start the PostgreSQL service:

sh

```
sudo service postgresql start
```

To create a new database user:

sh

```
sudo -u postgres createuser -s your_username
```

Set a password:

sh

```
sudo -u postgres psql
\password your_username
```

Installing MySQL

If you prefer **MySQL**, install it with:

- **macOS**:

    sh

    ```
    brew install mysql
    ```

- **Ubuntu/Debian**:

```sh
sh
```

```sh
sudo apt update
sudo apt install mysql-server
```

Start MySQL:

```sh
sh
```

```sh
sudo service mysql start
```

Create a database user:

```sql
sql
```

```sql
CREATE USER 'rails_user'@'localhost' IDENTIFIED
BY 'password';
GRANT    ALL    PRIVILEGES    ON    *.*    TO
'rails_user'@'localhost';
FLUSH PRIVILEGES;
```

2.4 Installing Essential Development Tools

1. Node.js and Yarn

Rails uses **Webpacker** to compile JavaScript assets, which
requires Node.js and Yarn.

- Install Node.js:

sh

```
brew install node  # macOS
sudo apt install nodejs npm  # Linux
```

- Install Yarn:

sh

```
npm install --global yarn
```

2. Git for Version Control

Git is essential for managing code changes and working in teams.

To install:

sh

```
sudo apt install git  # Linux
brew install git  # macOS
```

Verify installation:

sh

```
git --version
```

3. Rails CLI

Rails comes with a built-in command-line interface (CLI) to manage applications. To test:

```sh
```

```
rails new test_app
cd test_app
rails server
```

If everything is set up correctly, your Rails app should be running at:

```arduino
```

```
http://localhost:3000
```

Chapter Summary

Installed **Ruby** and **Rails** on different operating systems.
Learned how to **manage Ruby versions** using **RVM and rbenv**.
Set up **databases** (SQLite, PostgreSQL, MySQL).
Installed **essential development tools** like **Git, Node.js, and Yarn**.

49

Now that your development environment is ready, let's move to the **next chapter**, where we will explore the **Model-View-Controller (MVC) architecture in Rails** and why it's fundamental to building applications.

Next Chapter → Understanding MVC in Rails

CHAPTER 3

UNDERSTANDING MVC IN RAILS

Introduction

The **Model-View-Controller (MVC)** architecture is the foundation of Ruby on Rails. It helps **organize code**, separate concerns, and improve maintainability. Understanding how MVC works is essential for building scalable applications with Rails.

By the end of this chapter, you will: Understand **how MVC architecture works** in Rails. Learn **why the MVC pattern is beneficial** for web applications.

See **real-world examples of MVC in action**.

3.1 How Model-View-Controller (MVC) Architecture Works

What is MVC?

MVC is a **design pattern** that separates an application into three main components:

1. **Model** – Handles data and business logic.
2. **View** – Manages how information is displayed.
3. **Controller** – Acts as a bridge between the Model and View.

This separation helps in **organizing code efficiently** and **making maintenance easier**.

How MVC Works in Rails

In a Rails application, when a user makes a request (e.g., visiting a webpage), the following happens:

1. **User sends a request** (e.g., clicking on a link).
2. **The request is routed** to the correct **controller**.
3. **The controller interacts** with the **model** to get data.
4. **The controller sends data** to the **view** for presentation.
5. **The view generates HTML** and sends it back to the user.

This process ensures that the logic, data, and presentation are **separate and modular**.

Example of MVC in Action

Let's say we have a **blog application** where users can view posts.

- The **Model** (`Post` model) handles **database interactions**:

```ruby
class Post < ApplicationRecord
end
```

- The **Controller** (`PostsController`) fetches posts and **handles user actions**:

```ruby
class PostsController < ApplicationController
  def index
    @posts = Post.all  # Fetch all posts from the database
  end
end
```

- The **View** (`index.html.erb`) displays the posts:

```erb
<h1>All Blog Posts</h1>
```

53

```
<% @posts.each do |post| %>
  <h2><%= post.title %></h2>
  <p><%= post.body %></p>
<% end %>
```

When a user visits `http://localhost:3000/posts`:

1. **Rails routes the request** to `PostsController#index`.
2. **The controller fetches all posts** from the database.
3. **The view displays the posts** on the webpage.

This **clear separation of concerns** makes the code more structured and **easier to maintain**.

3.2 Benefits of the MVC Pattern

1. Separation of Concerns

- **Models handle data, controllers manage logic,** and **views display information**.
- This **keeps the codebase organized** and easier to work with.

2. Code Reusability

54

- Models, views, and controllers can be **reused** across different parts of the application.
- Example: The same **Post model** can be used in different controllers (e.g., `AdminPostsController` for managing posts in an admin panel).

3. Scalability and Maintainability

- Large applications remain **manageable** because responsibilities are divided.
- Developers can work on **different parts of the app** independently.

4. Easier Debugging and Testing

- Since logic, data, and presentation are separate, testing is more straightforward.
- Example: We can write **unit tests** for the model, **controller tests** for the logic, and **UI tests** for the view.

3.3 Examples of MVC in Action

Example 1: A Simple To-Do List

Model (`Task` model)

Handles data storage:

ruby

```ruby
class Task < ApplicationRecord
  validates :name, presence: true
end
```

Controller (`TasksController`)

Fetches data and interacts with the model:

ruby

```ruby
class TasksController < ApplicationController
  def index
    @tasks = Task.all
  end

  def new
    @task = Task.new
  end

  def create
    @task = Task.new(task_params)
    if @task.save
      redirect_to tasks_path
    else
```

56

```
      render :new
    end
  end


  private

  def task_params
    params.require(:task).permit(:name)
  end
end
```

View (index.html.erb)

Displays all tasks:

erb

```erb
<h1>My To-Do List</h1>
<% @tasks.each do |task| %>
  <p><%= task.name %></p>
<% end %>

<%= link_to "Add Task", new_task_path %>
```

☞ When a user visits /tasks:

- The **controller** fetches all tasks from the **model** and passes them to the **view**.
- The **view displays** the tasks on the webpage.

57

Example 2: A User Authentication System

Model (User model)

Stores user details:

ruby

```ruby
class User < ApplicationRecord
  has_secure_password
end
```
Controller (SessionsController)

Handles login and logout:

ruby

```ruby
class SessionsController < ApplicationController
  def create
    user = User.find_by(email: params[:email])
    if                    user                    &&
user.authenticate(params[:password])
      session[:user_id] = user.id
      redirect_to dashboard_path
    else
      flash[:error] = "Invalid email or password"
      render :new
```

```
    end
  end
end
```

View (new.html.erb)

Displays login form:

```erb
<h1>Login</h1>
<%= form_with url: login_path, method: :post do %>
  <%= label_tag :email %>
  <%= text_field_tag :email %>

  <%= label_tag :password %>
  <%= password_field_tag :password %>

  <%= submit_tag "Login" %>
<% end %>
```

☞ When a user submits the form:

- The **controller checks the credentials, authenticates the user,** and **creates a session**.
- The **view updates** to show the dashboard after a successful login.

Chapter Summary

MVC architecture separates concerns, improving organization and maintainability.
Models handle data, **controllers manage logic**, and **views control presentation**.
Rails enforces MVC by default, making it easy to build structured applications.
Examples (blog, to-do list, user authentication) demonstrate MVC in action.

In the next chapter, we'll **build our first Rails application from scratch**, creating models, controllers, and views.

Next Chapter → Your First Rails Application

CHAPTER 4

YOUR FIRST RAILS APPLICATION

Introduction

Now that we understand the **Model-View-Controller (MVC) architecture**, it's time to build our first Rails application. In this chapter, we'll create a basic Rails project, explore its folder structure, and run it for the first time.

By the end of this chapter, you will: Generate a new **Rails project** from scratch. Understand the **folder structure and key files**. Run a simple **Rails application locally**.

4.1 Generating a New Rails Project

Prerequisites

Before creating a Rails project, ensure you have:

- **Ruby installed** (`ruby -v` to check).
- **Rails installed** (`rails -v` to check).

- **A database (SQLite, PostgreSQL, or MySQL)** installed.

Creating a New Rails Application

To generate a new Rails project, use the following command:

```sh

rails new my_first_app
```

This command:

- Creates a new folder named `my_first_app`.
- Sets up the **default folder structure** for a Rails app.
- Installs dependencies and initializes a **Git repository** (if Git is installed).

Choosing a Database

By default, Rails uses **SQLite**, but you can specify a different database:

- **For PostgreSQL:**

```sh
```

```
rails        new       my_first_app        --
database=postgresql
```

- **For MySQL:**

```
sh
```

```
rails new my_first_app --database=mysql
```

Move into your project directory:

```
sh
```

```
cd my_first_app
```

4.2 Folder Structure and Key Files

After running the `rails new` command, Rails creates a structured set of folders and files:

```
lua
```

```
my_first_app/
|-- app/
|    ├── controllers/
|    ├── models/
|    ├── views/
|    ├── helpers/
|    ├── assets/
```

```
|-- bin/
|-- config/
|-- db/
|-- lib/
|-- log/
|-- public/
|-- test/
|-- tmp/
|-- vendor/
|-- Gemfile
|-- Rakefile
|-- config.ru
|-- README.md
```

Important Folders and Files

Folder/File	Description
`app/`	The heart of the application. Contains MVC components.
`app/controllers/`	Houses controllers that handle user requests.
`app/models/`	Stores models that interact with the database.

Folder/File	Description
app/views/	Contains HTML templates for rendering UI.
config/	Stores application settings and routing rules.
db/	Holds database migration files.
public/	Stores static files like error pages and assets.
Gemfile	Defines dependencies required for the project.
Rakefile	Automates tasks like database migrations.

4.3 Running a Simple Rails App

Step 1: Start the Rails Server

Inside your project directory, run:

```sh
rails server
```

or

```
sh
```

```
rails s
```

You should see output like:

```
java
```

```
=> Booting Puma
=> Rails 7.0.4 application starting in
development mode
=> Listening on http://127.0.0.1:3000
```

This means your application is running. Open **http://localhost:3000** in your web browser, and you should see the Rails welcome page.

Step 2: Creating a Simple Page

Let's create a basic page by adding a new controller.

```
sh
```

```
rails generate controller Pages home
```

This   command:

Creates a **controller** named `PagesController.`

Generates a **view** **file** at `app/views/pages/home.html.erb`.

Adds a **route** in `config/routes.rb`.

Step 3: Define a Route

Open `config/routes.rb` and modify it to:

```ruby
Rails.application.routes.draw do
  root "pages#home"
end
```

This sets the home page of your application to **PagesController's home action**.

Step 4: Edit the View

Now, edit `app/views/pages/home.html.erb` and add:

```erb
<h1>Welcome to My First Rails App</h1>
<p>This is a simple Rails application!</p>
```

Step 5: Restart the Server

Restart the Rails server:

```sh
```

```
rails s
```

Now, when you visit **http://localhost:3000**, you'll see the custom homepage.

Chapter Summary

Generated a new Rails project with `rails new`. **Explored the folder structure** and key files in a Rails app. **Started the Rails server** and accessed the application. **Created a simple home page** using controllers, views, and routes.

Now that we have our first application running, in the next chapter, we'll explore **Routing and Controllers** in more detail.

Next Chapter → Routing and Controllers in Rails

CHAPTER 5

ROUTING AND CONTROLLERS IN RAILS

Introduction

Routing and controllers are essential components of a Rails application. The **router** directs incoming requests to the appropriate **controller action**, which processes the request and sends back a response.

By the end of this chapter, you will:
Understand **how Rails routes work** and define custom routes.

Learn how to **create and manage controllers** in a Rails app.

Explore **how controllers handle requests and responses** effectively.

5.1 How Rails Routes Work

What is a Route?

A **route** in Rails maps a URL to a specific **controller action**. When a user visits a URL (e.g., `http://localhost:3000/posts`), Rails checks the **routes file (`config/routes.rb`)** to determine **which controller and action** should handle the request.

Defining Routes in Rails

Routes are defined in `config/routes.rb`. Here's an example:

ruby

```
Rails.application.routes.draw do
  get 'posts', to: 'posts#index'
end
```

This means:

- A **GET request** to `/posts` will be handled by `PostsController#index`.

Types of Routes in Rails

Route Type	Syntax	Example	Maps To
GET	`get 'path', to: 'controller#action'`	`get 'posts', to: 'posts#index'`	Fetches data
POST	`post 'path', to: 'controller#action'`	`post 'posts', to: 'posts#create'`	Submits data
PUT/PATCH	`put 'path', to: 'controller#action'`	`put 'posts/:id', to: 'posts#update'`	Updates data
DELETE	`delete 'path', to: 'controller#action'`	`delete 'posts/:id', to: 'posts#destroy'`	Deletes data

RESTful Routes

Rails follows the **REST (Representational State Transfer) architecture**, which provides **seven standard routes** for resources:

ruby

```
resources :posts
```

This single line generates:

sh

```
GET     /posts          → posts#index
GET     /posts/new      → posts#new
POST    /posts          → posts#create
GET     /posts/:id      → posts#show
GET     /posts/:id/edit → posts#edit
PATCH   /posts/:id      → posts#update
DELETE  /posts/:id      → posts#destroy
```

To view all routes in a Rails app, run:

sh

```
rails routes
```

5.2 Creating and Managing Controllers

What is a Controller?

A **controller** is responsible for: **Processing user requests**. **Retrieving data** from the model. **Passing data** to the view for rendering.

Generating a Controller

To create a new controller:

sh

```
rails generate controller Posts
```

This generates:

- A **controller file**: `app/controllers/posts_controller.rb`
- A **view folder**: `app/views/posts/`
- A **routes entry** in `config/routes.rb`

Basic Controller Actions

Inside `app/controllers/posts_controller.rb`, we define actions:

```ruby
ruby

class PostsController < ApplicationController
  def index
    @posts = Post.all
  end

  def show
    @post = Post.find(params[:id])
  end
end
```

Strong Parameters for Security

When creating or updating records, we use **strong parameters** to prevent mass assignment vulnerabilities:

```ruby
ruby

private

def post_params
  params.require(:post).permit(:title, :body)
end
```

5.3 Handling Requests and Responses

How a Controller Handles a Request

74

When a request is made, Rails follows these steps:

1. **Routes direct the request** to the right controller action.
2. **The controller processes data** (fetching from the model).
3. **The controller passes data** to the view.
4. **The view renders a response** to the user.

Example: Handling a Request

Let's assume we have a `PostsController`:

ruby

```
class PostsController < ApplicationController
  def index
    @posts = Post.all
    render :index
  end
end
```

- `@posts = Post.all` → Fetches all posts from the database.
- `render :index` → Sends data to app/views/posts/index.html.erb.

Handling JSON Responses

75

Rails can return JSON responses instead of HTML:

ruby

```
class PostsController < ApplicationController
  def index
    @posts = Post.all
    render json: @posts
  end
end
```

Now, visiting /posts will return **JSON data** instead of a webpage.

Redirecting Users

To redirect users to another page:

ruby

```
def create
  @post = Post.new(post_params)
  if @post.save
    redirect_to  posts_path,  notice:  "Post
created successfully!"
  else
    render :new
  end
end
```

- `redirect_to` → Sends users to another page.
- `render` → Displays a template without redirecting.

Chapter Summary

Routes map URLs to controller actions. Controllers handle user requests and process data. Responses can be HTML or JSON, with redirects as needed.

In the next chapter, we'll explore **Active Record and how Rails interacts with databases.**

Next Chapter → Active Record: The Heart of Rails

CHAPTER 6

ACTIVE RECORD – THE HEART OF RAILS

Introduction

One of Rails' most powerful features is **Active Record**, which serves as the **Object-Relational Mapping (ORM)** layer. Active Record allows developers to interact with the database **without writing raw SQL queries**.

By the end of this chapter, you will: Understand **ORM (Object-Relational Mapping)** and how Rails uses Active Record. Learn about **migrations, schema, and database management** in Rails. Create and manage **models** to store and retrieve data efficiently.

6.1 ORM and Database Interactions

What is ORM?

Object-Relational Mapping (ORM) is a technique that allows developers to interact with databases using **objects** instead of SQL queries.

In traditional SQL, fetching all users looks like this:

```sql
sql

SELECT * FROM users;
```

With Active Record in Rails, we can do the same with:

```ruby
ruby

User.all
```

☞ This approach makes database interactions **more intuitive and readable**.

How Active Record Works

Active Record **maps database tables to Ruby classes**, allowing us to work with records as objects.

Database Table Active Record Model

users table   User model (app/models/user.rb)

posts table   Post model (app/models/post.rb)

Active Record automatically translates method calls into SQL queries.

For example:

ruby

```
User.find(1)   # Fetches user with ID = 1
```

translates to:

sql

```
SELECT * FROM users WHERE id = 1;
```

6.2 Migrations, Schema, and Database Management

What is a Migration?

A **migration** in Rails is a way to modify the database schema using Ruby code instead of raw SQL.

Creating a Migration

To create a new migration, run:

```sh
```

```sh
rails generate migration CreateUsers
```

This generates a file in `db/migrate/`, such as:

```ruby
```

```ruby
class CreateUsers < ActiveRecord::Migration[7.0]
  def change
    create_table :users do |t|
      t.string :name
      t.string :email
      t.timestamps
    end
  end
end
```

This code: Creates a `users` table. Adds `name` and `email` columns. Adds **timestamps** (`created_at` and `updated_at`).

To apply the migration, run:

```sh
```

81

```
rails db:migrate
```

Understanding the Schema

The **schema file (db/schema.rb)** reflects the current database structure.

Example schema:

ruby

```ruby
ActiveRecord::Schema.define(version:
20240305123000) do
  create_table "users", force: :cascade do |t|
    t.string "name"
    t.string "email"
    t.datetime "created_at", null: false
    t.datetime "updated_at", null: false
  end
end
```

Rolling Back Migrations

If you make a mistake in a migration, you can roll it back:

sh

```
rails db:rollback
```

To undo **multiple migrations**:

```
sh
```

```
rails db:rollback STEP=2
```

To reset and rerun all migrations:

```
sh
```

```
rails db:reset
```

6.3 Creating and Managing Models

What is a Model?

A **model** represents a database table in Rails. It contains logic for interacting with database records.

Generating a Model

To create a `User` model:

```
sh
```

```
rails    generate    model    User    name:string
email:string
```

This creates:

- A migration file in `db/migrate/`
- A model file in `app/models/user.rb`

Defining Validations

Validations ensure data integrity. For example:

```ruby
ruby
```

```ruby
class User < ApplicationRecord
  validates :name, presence: true
  validates :email, presence: true, uniqueness:
true
end
```

Now, trying to create a user **without a name** will fail:

```ruby
ruby
```

```ruby
User.create(name: "", email: "test@example.com")
# Output: Validation failed: Name can't be blank
```

Querying the Database with Active Record

Active Record provides **methods for querying the database**.

Task	Active Record Query
Retrieve all users	`User.all`
Find a user by ID	`User.find(1)`
Find a user by email	`User.find_by(email: "test@example.com")`
Get users with a condition	`User.where("name LIKE ?", "%John%")`
Order users by name	`User.order(:name)`
Limit the number of records	`User.limit(5)`
Delete a user	`User.destroy(1)`

Adding Associations

Rails models can be **associated** with each other.

One-to-Many Relationship

A **user** can have many **posts**:

ruby

```ruby
class User < ApplicationRecord
  has_many :posts
end

class Post < ApplicationRecord
  belongs_to :user
end
```

With this setup, you can now:

ruby

```ruby
user = User.first
user.posts.create(title: "My first post", body: "Hello, world!")
```

Many-to-Many Relationship

Users can have **many roles**, and roles can belong to **many users**:

ruby

```ruby
class User < ApplicationRecord
```

```
  has_and_belongs_to_many :roles
end

class Role < ApplicationRecord
  has_and_belongs_to_many :users
end
```

Seeding the Database

Seeding allows us to **prepopulate** the database with sample data.

Modify db/seeds.rb:

ruby

```
User.create(name:    "John    Doe",    email:
"john@example.com")
User.create(name:    "Jane    Doe",    email:
"jane@example.com")
```

Run:

sh

```
rails db:seed
```

Chapter Summary

Active Record provides an intuitive way to interact with databases.

Migrations help modify database schema without raw SQL.

Models represent database tables and include validations, associations, and queries.

Seeding prepopulates the database with initial data.

In the next chapter, we'll explore **associations and validations in more detail**.

Next Chapter → Associations and Validations in Rails

CHAPTER 7: ASSOCIATIONS AND VALIDATIONS IN RAILS

Introduction

Building relationships between models is a fundamental part of web development. Rails provides **associations** to define relationships between database tables and **validations** to enforce data integrity.

By the end of this chapter, you will:
Understand **one-to-many** and **many-to-many** relationships in Rails.
Learn how to **implement validations and constraints** to maintain data integrity.
Use **Active Record callbacks** to execute logic at specific moments in a record's lifecycle.

7.1 One-to-Many and Many-to-Many Relationships

What Are Associations?

Associations define **how models are related**. Rails supports **three types of relationships**:

Association Type	Example	Model Setup
One-to-One	A user has one profile	`has_one`
One-to-Many	A user has many posts	`has_many` / `belongs_to`
Many-to-Many	A user has many roles, and roles belong to many users	`has_and_belongs_to_many` / `has_many :through`

One-to-Many Relationship

Example: A **user** has many **posts**, and a **post** belongs to a **user**.

Step 1: Generate Models

```sh
rails generate model User name:string email:string
```

```
rails generate model Post title:string body:text
user:references
rails db:migrate
```

Step 2: Define the Relationship

Modify `app/models/user.rb`:

ruby

```ruby
class User < ApplicationRecord
  has_many :posts, dependent: :destroy
end
```

Modify `app/models/post.rb`:

ruby

```ruby
class Post < ApplicationRecord
  belongs_to :user
end
```

☞ **What happens here?**

- A `User` **has many** `Post` records.
- A `Post` **belongs to** a `User`.
- `dependent: :destroy` ensures that **when a user is deleted, all their posts are deleted too**.

Step 3: Using the Association

ruby

```
user   =   User.create(name:   "Alice",   email:
"alice@example.com")
user.posts.create(title:   "First   Post",   body:
"Hello,  world!")
```

To fetch all posts of a user:

ruby

```
user.posts
```

To find the user who wrote a post:

ruby

```
post = Post.first
post.user
```

Many-to-Many   Relationship
(has_and_belongs_to_many)

Example: A **user** can have many **roles**, and a **role** can belong to many **users**.

92

Step 1: Generate Models

sh

```
rails generate model Role name:string
rails generate model UserRole user:references
role:references
rails db:migrate
```

Step 2: Define the Relationship

Modify app/models/user.rb:

ruby

```
class User < ApplicationRecord
  has_many :user_roles
  has_many :roles, through: :user_roles
end
```

Modify app/models/role.rb:

ruby

```
class Role < ApplicationRecord
  has_many :user_roles
  has_many :users, through: :user_roles
end
```

Modify app/models/user_role.rb:

ruby

```
class UserRole < ApplicationRecord
  belongs_to :user
  belongs_to :role
end
```

Step 3: Using the Association

ruby

```
admin = Role.create(name: "Admin")
user = User.create(name: "Bob", email:
"bob@example.com")
user.roles << admin
```

To check a user's roles:

ruby

```
user.roles
```

☞ This structure is more flexible than
has_and_belongs_to_many, as it allows **additional
attributes** like timestamps in user_roles.

7.2 Implementing Validations and Constraints

Why Use Validations?

Validations ensure that **data is correct** before saving it to the database.

Common Validations in Rails

Validation Type	Example
`presence: true`	Ensures a field is not empty.
`uniqueness: true`	Prevents duplicate records.
`length: { minimum: X }`	Enforces minimum/maximum length.
`format: { with: REGEX }`	Validates format (e.g., email).
`numericality: true`	Ensures a field contains a number.

Adding Validations to a Model

Modify `app/models/user.rb`:

ruby

```ruby
class User < ApplicationRecord
  validates :name, presence: true
```

95

```
validates :email, presence: true, uniqueness:
true, format: { with: URI::MailTo::EMAIL_REGEXP
}
end
```

☞ Now, trying to create an invalid user:

ruby

```
User.create(name: "", email: "not_an_email")
```

Rails will return:

rust

```
Validation failed: Name can't be blank, Email is
invalid
```

Database-Level Constraints

Rails **validations happen at the application level**, but **database constraints enforce rules at the database level**.

Example: Add **NOT NULL constraints** in a migration:

ruby

```
class          AddConstraintsToUsers          <
ActiveRecord::Migration[7.0]
  def change
    change_column_null :users, :name, false
    add_index :users, :email, unique: true
  end
end
```

☞ This ensures:

- name **cannot be NULL** at the database level.
- email **must be unique**.

Run the migration:

```sh
sh
```

```
rails db:migrate
```

7.3 Using Active Record Callbacks

What Are Callbacks?

Active Record callbacks allow us to **execute logic at specific points** in a record's lifecycle.

Callback	Description
before_validation	Runs before validations are checked.
after_validation	Runs after validations pass.
before_save	Runs before the record is saved.
after_save	Runs after the record is saved.
before_create	Runs before a new record is created.
after_create	Runs after a new record is created.
before_update	Runs before an existing record is updated.
after_update	Runs after an existing record is updated.
before_destroy	Runs before a record is deleted.
after_destroy	Runs after a record is deleted.

Example: Automatically Capitalizing a User's Name

Modify app/models/user.rb:

ruby

```ruby
class User < ApplicationRecord
  before_save :capitalize_name

  validates :name, presence: true

  private

  def capitalize_name
    self.name = name.capitalize
  end
end
```

Now:

ruby

```ruby
user = User.create(name: "alice", email: "alice@example.com")
puts user.name  # Output: "Alice"
```

Example: Sending a Welcome Email After a User is Created

ruby

```ruby
class User < ApplicationRecord
```

```
after_create :send_welcome_email

private

def send_welcome_email
  puts "Sending welcome email to
#{self.email}..."
  # Code to send email goes here
end
end
```

Now, when a user is created:

```ruby
```

```
User.create(name: "Alice", email:
"alice@example.com")
```

The console will output:

```css
```

```
Sending welcome email to alice@example.com...
```

☞ Callbacks help **automate actions** like formatting data, sending notifications, and maintaining data integrity.

Chapter Summary

One-to-many and many-to-many relationships allow flexible data structuring.
Validations prevent bad data from entering the database.
Active Record callbacks automate tasks like formatting, sending emails, and logging actions.

In the next chapter, we'll explore **seeding and querying data efficiently** in Rails.

Next Chapter → Seeding and Querying Data in Rails

CHAPTER 8

SEEDING AND QUERYING DATA IN RAILS

Introduction

Seeding and querying data are essential skills in Rails development. **Seeding** helps populate the database with test data, while **querying** enables efficient data retrieval using Active Record. In this chapter, we'll cover how to:

 Populate the database with **seed data** for testing and development.

Write **Active Record queries** to retrieve data efficiently.

Optimize queries for **better performance**.

8.1 Populating the Database with Seed Data

Why Use Seed Data?

Seed data helps:

- **Prepopulate** the database with test records.

- **Develop and test features** without manually entering data.
- **Simulate real-world scenarios** before deploying the app.

Using the `db/seeds.rb` File

Rails provides a **`db/seeds.rb`** file to add initial records.

Example: Seeding **Users** and **Posts**

Modify db/seeds.rb:

ruby

```
# Clear existing records
User.destroy_all
Post.destroy_all

# Create users
users = []
5.times do |i|
  users << User.create(name: "User#{i+1}",
email: "user#{i+1}@example.com")
end

# Create posts for each user
users.each do |user|
  3.times do
```

```
    user.posts.create(title:    "Sample    Post",
body: "This is a test post.")
  end
end


puts "Database seeded successfully!"
```

☞   This   script:

Deletes existing records before inserting new ones.

Creates   **5**   **users**.

Each user has **3 posts**.

Running the Seed File

Execute the seed file with:

sh

```
rails db:seed
```

Now, check the database:

sh

```
rails console
User.count   # Should return 5
Post.count   # Should return 15
```

Using `Faker` for Realistic Data

Instead of using static data, we can use the **Faker** gem to generate random values.

Step 1: Install the Faker Gem

Add this to your `Gemfile`:

```ruby
gem 'faker'
```

Run:

```sh
bundle install
```

Step 2: Modify `db/seeds.rb`

```ruby
require 'faker'

User.destroy_all
Post.destroy_all

10.times do
  user = User.create(
    name: Faker::Name.name,
```

```
    email: Faker::Internet.email
  )

  5.times do
    user.posts.create(
      title: Faker::Book.title,
      body: Faker::Lorem.paragraph
    )
  end
end

puts "Seed data created successfully!"
```

☞ Now, the database will have **random names, emails, and post titles**, making the app feel more realistic.

8.2 Writing Queries Using Active Record

Basic Active Record Queries

Active Record makes querying simple and readable.

Query	Active Record Code
Get all users	`User.all`

106

Query	Active Record Code
Find a user by ID	`User.find(1)`
Find by attribute	`User.find_by(email: "test@example.com")`
Get users with a condition	`User.where("name LIKE ?", "%John%")`
Order records	`User.order(:name)`
Limit results	`User.limit(5)`
Count records	`User.count`
Delete a record	`User.destroy(1)`

Using Query Chains

Rails allows **chaining multiple queries** together.

Example: Get the **latest 5 posts** from a specific user:

```ruby
```

```
User.find_by(email:
"user@example.com").posts.order(created_at:
:desc).limit(5)
```

This translates to:

```sql
sql

SELECT * FROM posts
WHERE user_id = (SELECT id FROM users WHERE email
= "user@example.com")
ORDER BY created_at DESC
LIMIT 5;
```

☞ **Chaining queries** makes the code **clean and efficient**.

Querying Related Models

Using associations, we can retrieve related records efficiently.

Example: Get **all posts written by a specific user**:

```ruby
ruby

user = User.find(1)
user.posts
```

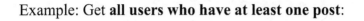

Example: Get **all users who have at least one post**:

ruby

```
User.joins(:posts).distinct
```

Example: Get **posts with more than 100 likes** (assuming a likes_count column exists):

ruby

```
Post.where("likes_count > ?", 100)
```

8.3 Optimizing Queries for Performance

1. Using select to Fetch Only Needed Fields

By default, Active Record retrieves **all columns**. To improve performance, select only the fields you need.

Instead of:

ruby

```
User.all
```

Use:

```ruby

User.select(:id, :name)
```

☞ This reduces **database load** and **improves response time**.

---

2. Avoiding N+1 Queries with `includes` and `joins`

What is the N+1 Query Problem?

Consider this loop:

```ruby

users = User.all
users.each do |user|
  puts user.posts.count
end
```

● **Problem:** This runs **one query for users + one query for each user's posts**, leading to **N+1 queries**.

 Solution: Use `includes`

```ruby

```

```
users = User.includes(:posts)
users.each do |user|
  puts user.posts.count
end
```

This **preloads posts** in one query:

sql

```
SELECT * FROM users;
SELECT * FROM posts WHERE user_id IN (1,2,3,4,5);
```

☞ `includes` **improves efficiency** by **reducing queries**.

---

3. Indexing for Faster Queries

Adding **indexes** improves performance for frequently searched fields.

To index the `email` column:

sh

```
rails generate migration AddIndexToUsersEmail
```

Modify the migration file:

```ruby
ruby
```

```ruby
class          AddIndexToUsersEmail          <
ActiveRecord::Migration[7.0]
  def change
    add_index :users, :email, unique: true
  end
end
```

Run:

```sh
sh
```

```sh
rails db:migrate
```

☞ **Indexed fields** make lookups **significantly faster**.

---

4. Using `find_each` for Large Datasets

Loading thousands of records at once **consumes too much memory**.

✘ Avoid this:

```ruby
ruby
```

```ruby
User.all.each do |user|
```

```
  process(user)
end
```

Use `find_each` instead:

ruby

```
User.find_each do |user|
  process(user)
end
```

☞ This **loads records in batches**, reducing **memory usage**.

---

5. Caching Query Results

If a query runs **frequently, cache the result** to prevent unnecessary database hits.

Example:

ruby

```
Rails.cache.fetch("top_users",        expires_in:
10.minutes) do
  User.order(points: :desc).limit(5)
end
```

☞ **Caching speeds up response times** and **reduces database workload**.

Chapter Summary

Seeding populates the database with test data using `db/seeds.rb`.

Active Record makes querying easy with readable syntax.

Optimizing queries with `select`, `includes`, indexing, and caching improves performance.

In the next chapter, we'll explore **working with external APIs and integrating third-party services in Rails**.

Next Chapter → Working with External APIs and Third-Party Services

CHAPTER 9

WORKING WITH EXTERNAL APIS AND THIRD-PARTY SERVICES

Introduction

Modern web applications often rely on **external APIs** and **third-party services** for data, payments, authentication, and more. Rails provides built-in tools and gems to integrate these services seamlessly.

By the end of this chapter, you will: Learn how to **consume APIs in Rails** using HTTP requests. Use **gems** to simplify API integrations. Implement **OAuth authentication** to allow users to log in with third-party providers like Google and GitHub.

9.1 Consuming APIs with Rails

What is an API?

An **API (Application Programming Interface)** allows applications to communicate with each other. Common APIs include:

- **Weather APIs** (e.g., OpenWeatherMap)
- **Payment APIs** (e.g., Stripe, PayPal)
- **Social Media APIs** (e.g., Twitter, Facebook)

Making API Requests with `Net::HTTP`

Rails provides the `Net::HTTP` library for making API calls.

Example: Fetching weather data from OpenWeatherMap.

Step 1: Get an API Key

Sign up at OpenWeatherMap and get an API key.

Step 2: Make a Request

Modify `app/services/weather_service.rb`:

ruby

```
require 'net/http'
require 'json'
```

116

```ruby
class WeatherService
  BASE_URL                                    =
"https://api.openweathermap.org/data/2.5/weathe
r"

  def self.get_weather(city)
    url                                       =
URI("#{BASE_URL}?q=#{city}&appid=YOUR_API_KEY&u
nits=metric")
    response = Net::HTTP.get(url)
    JSON.parse(response)
  end
end
```

Step 3: Use in a Controller

Modify app/controllers/weather_controller.rb:

ruby

```ruby
class WeatherController < ApplicationController
  def show
    @weather                                  =
WeatherService.get_weather(params[:city])
  end
end
```

Step 4: Display in a View

Modify app/views/weather/show.html.erb:

117

erb

```
<h1>Weather in <%= @weather["name"] %></h1>
<p>Temperature:  <%=  @weather["main"]["temp"]
%>°C</p>
<p>Condition:                        <%=
@weather["weather"].first["description"] %></p>
```

Using HTTParty for API Requests

Instead of Net::HTTP, we can use the **HTTParty gem** for simpler API requests.

Step 1: Install HTTParty

Add to Gemfile:

ruby

```
gem 'httparty'
```

Run:

sh

```
bundle install
```

Step 2: Modify API Service

ruby

```
require 'httparty'

class WeatherService
  include HTTParty
  base_uri
'https://api.openweathermap.org/data/2.5'

  def self.get_weather(city)
    get("/weather", query: { q: city, appid:
"YOUR_API_KEY", units: "metric" })
  end
end
```

☞ This simplifies API calls by **removing manual request handling**.

9.2 Using Gems for API Integration

Many services provide **gems** for easy integration.

Example 1: Integrating Stripe for Payments

Stripe is a popular payment gateway.

Step 1: Install Stripe Gem

Add to `Gemfile`:

ruby

```
gem 'stripe'
```

Run:

sh

```
bundle install
```

Step 2: Configure Stripe in Rails

Create a new initializer:

sh

```
touch config/initializers/stripe.rb
```

Modify `config/initializers/stripe.rb`:

ruby

```
Stripe.api_key = "YOUR_SECRET_KEY"
```

Step 3: Charge a Customer

Modify `app/controllers/payments_controller.rb`:

120

ruby

```
class PaymentsController < ApplicationController
  def create
    charge = Stripe::Charge.create({
      amount: 5000, # Amount in cents ($50)
      currency: "usd",
      source: params[:stripeToken],
      description: "Test Charge"
    })

    render json: { status: "Payment successful!"
}
  rescue Stripe::CardError => e
    render json: { error: e.message }, status:
:unprocessable_entity
  end
end
```

☞ Now, users can **make payments** using Stripe!

Example 2: Sending Emails with SendGrid

Step 1: Install SendGrid Gem

ruby

```
gem 'sendgrid-ruby'
```

Run:

sh

```
bundle install
```

Step 2: Configure SendGrid API Key

Create config/initializers/sendgrid.rb:

ruby

```
SendGrid.api_key = ENV['SENDGRID_API_KEY']
```

Step 3: Send an Email

Modify app/mailers/user_mailer.rb:

ruby

```
class UserMailer < ApplicationMailer
  def welcome_email(user)
    mail(to: user.email, subject: "Welcome to Our
App!", body: "Thanks for signing up!")
  end
end
```

Now, we can send emails using:

ruby

```
UserMailer.welcome_email(User.first).deliver_no
w
```

☞ **Using gems simplifies API interactions**.

9.3 OAuth and Authentication with Third-Party Services

What is OAuth?

OAuth allows users to **log in with third-party providers** like Google, GitHub, or Facebook.

Using OmniAuth for Google Authentication

Step 1: Install OmniAuth Gem

Add to `Gemfile`:

```ruby

gem 'omniauth-google-oauth2'
```

Run:

```sh

bundle install
```

Step 2: Configure OmniAuth

Modify `config/initializers/omniauth.rb`:

ruby

```ruby
Rails.application.config.middleware.use
OmniAuth::Builder do
  provider  :google_oauth2,  "GOOGLE_CLIENT_ID",
"GOOGLE_CLIENT_SECRET"
end
```

Step 3: Create an OAuth Callback Controller

Modify `app/controllers/sessions_controller.rb`:

ruby

```ruby
class SessionsController < ApplicationController
  def google_auth
    user_info                                =
request.env['omniauth.auth']['info']
    user    =    User.find_or_create_by(email:
user_info['email']) do |u|
      u.name = user_info['name']
      u.password = SecureRandom.hex(16)
    end
    session[:user_id] = user.id
    redirect_to  root_path,  notice:  "Signed  in
successfully!"
```

```
  end
end
```

Step 4: Update Routes

Modify `config/routes.rb`:

```ruby
get        '/auth/:provider/callback',        to:
'sessions#google_auth'
```

☞ Now, users can **log in with Google** by visiting
`/auth/google_oauth2`.

Chapter Summary

Consuming APIs in Rails using `Net::HTTP` and `HTTParty`.
Using gems to simplify API integrations (e.g., Stripe, SendGrid).
Implementing OAuth authentication with Google via OmniAuth.

In the next chapter, we'll explore **views, templating, and front-end integration in Rails**.

125

Next Chapter → Views and Front-End Integration in Rails

CHAPTER 10

ERB, HAML, AND SLIM – TEMPLATING IN RAILS

Introduction

In Rails, views handle the **presentation layer** of your application. They display the data passed from the controller and provide the interface through which users interact with the app. To make the view layer efficient and maintainable, Rails offers several **template engines** to choose from. In this chapter, we'll explore the popular templating engines: **ERB**, **Haml**, and **Slim**.

By the end of this chapter, you will: Understand the differences between **ERB**, **Haml**, and **Slim**. Learn how to write **dynamic views** to display data. Use **partials and layouts** to avoid repetition and structure your views efficiently.

10.1 Choosing the Right Template Engine

What is a Template Engine?

A **template engine** is a tool that converts **HTML files** embedded with **Ruby code** into dynamic web pages. The Ruby code is evaluated and replaced with actual data, creating **dynamic views**.

Rails comes with **ERB (Embedded Ruby)** as the default template engine, but you can also use **Haml** and **Slim**, both of which provide cleaner and more concise syntax.

ERB (Embedded Ruby)

ERB is the default templating engine in Rails. It allows you to mix Ruby code within HTML using <%= %> tags.

Example of ERB Syntax:

```
erb
```

```
<h1>Welcome, <%= @user.name %></h1>
<p>Your email: <%= @user.email %></p>
```

- <%= %>: **Evaluates Ruby code and outputs the result** to the page.
- <% %>: **Executes Ruby code without outputting it** (e.g., loops).

Pros of ERB

- **Default in Rails** – No setup required.
- **Widely supported** and familiar to most Rails developers.

Cons of ERB

- Can be **verbose** for complex HTML structures with embedded Ruby.

Haml (HTML Abstraction Markup Language)

Haml offers a **cleaner, more concise syntax** that eliminates the need for closing tags and Ruby delimiters like <%= %>.

Example of Haml Syntax:

```haml
%h1 Welcome, #{@user.name}
%p Your email: #{@user.email}
```

- %h1, %p: Represents HTML tags (<h1>, <p>, etc.).
- @user.name: Directly accesses Ruby variables in the template.

Pros of Haml

- **Cleaner syntax** with less clutter.
- Eliminates repetitive HTML closing tags.
- Easy to read and maintain.

Cons of Haml

- Requires installation and configuration in a Rails app.
- **Not as widely used** as ERB, so learning resources are less abundant.

How to Use Haml in Rails

Add Haml to your `Gemfile`:

```ruby
gem 'haml-rails'
```

Run:

```sh
bundle install
```

Then, change `.erb` files to `.haml` for your views.

Slim

Slim is another templating engine that emphasizes **minimalist syntax** and **high performance**. Like Haml, Slim removes redundant HTML tags and Ruby delimiters.

Example of Slim Syntax:
```slim

h1 Welcome, #{@user.name}
p Your email: #{@user.email}
```

- No percentage signs or @ symbols, resulting in the **smallest syntax** possible.

Pros of Slim

- **Very concise and fast** compared to Haml.
- Offers a clean, readable syntax that is easy to maintain.

Cons of Slim

- Like Haml, Slim **requires installation** and setup in Rails.
- **Smaller community** than ERB, making support harder to find.

How to Use Slim in Rails

Add Slim to your `Gemfile`:

```ruby
```

```
gem 'slim-rails'
```

Run:

```sh
```

```
bundle install
```

Change `.erb` files to `.slim` to use Slim for your views.

10.2 Writing Dynamic Views

Displaying Dynamic Data in Views

Dynamic views display content passed from controllers. For instance, to show a list of users, you can loop through the `@users` instance variable and display each one:

ERB Example:

```erb
```

```
<h1>All Users</h1>
<ul>
  <% @users.each do |user| %>
    <li><%= user.name %> - <%= user.email %></li>
  <% end %>
</ul>
```

Haml Example:

haml

```
%h1 All Users
%ul
  - @users.each do |user|
    %li= user.name + " - " + user.email
```

Slim Example:

slim

```
h1 All Users
ul
  - @users.each do |user|
    li = user.name + " - " + user.email
```

Each example uses Ruby code to dynamically output user information.

Using Conditionals in Views

You can also use **conditionals** to display content based on certain conditions.

ERB Example:

erb

```
<% if @user.admin? %>
  <p>Welcome, admin!</p>
<% else %>
  <p>Welcome, regular user!</p>
<% end %>
```

Haml Example:

haml

```
- if @user.admin?
  %p Welcome, admin!
- else
  %p Welcome, regular user!
```

Slim Example:

slim

```
- if @user.admin?
  p Welcome, admin!
- else
  p Welcome, regular user!
```

10.3 Using Partials and Layouts

Partials

Partials are reusable pieces of HTML code that can be included in multiple views to avoid repetition. For example, if you want to display a user's profile information across different pages, you can create a partial.

Creating a Partial

Create a partial in `app/views/users/_profile.html.erb`:

erb

```erb
<div class="profile">
  <h2><%= @user.name %></h2>
  <p><%= @user.email %></p>
</div>
```

To render this partial in a view:

erb

```erb
<%= render 'users/profile' %>
```

Rails automatically looks for `_profile.html.erb` and includes it in the view.

Partials in Haml and Slim

- **Haml:**

  ```
  haml
  ```

  ```
  = render 'users/profile'
  ```

- **Slim:**

  ```
  slim
  ```

  ```
  = render 'users/profile'
  ```

Layouts

Layouts allow you to define a consistent structure for your pages, such as headers, footers, and navigation menus. Rails provides a default layout (`app/views/layouts/application.html.erb`) that wraps around all views.

Modifying the Default Layout

Modify the default layout (`app/views/layouts/application.html.erb`) to include a header and footer:

```
erb

<!DOCTYPE html>
<html>
<head>
  <title>MyApp</title>
</head>
<body>
  <header>
    <h1>Welcome to MyApp</h1>
    <nav>
      <%= link_to 'Home', root_path %>
      <%= link_to 'About', about_path %>
    </nav>
  </header>

  <%= yield %>  <!-- This is where the content of
each page will be inserted -->

  <footer>
    <p>&; 2025 MyApp</p>
  </footer>
</body>
</html>
```

Using Different Layouts for Specific Actions

You can define different layouts for specific controllers or actions:

ruby

```
class UsersController < ApplicationController
  layout "user_layout", only: [:show]
end
```

Chapter Summary

ERB, **Haml**, and **Slim** are the main templating engines used in   Rails.

Use **partials** to avoid repetition and make views more maintainable.

Layouts allow you to create consistent structures across multiple pages.

In the next chapter, we'll explore **front-end integration** in Rails using tools like Webpacker, Bootstrap, and JavaScript frameworks.

Next Chapter → Front-End Integration in Rails

CHAPTER 11

FRONT-END INTEGRATION WITH RAILS

Introduction

Front-end integration is a crucial part of building modern web applications. Rails provides several tools to seamlessly integrate popular front-end frameworks like **Bootstrap**, **Tailwind CSS**, and **Vue.js**. Additionally, managing assets and handling JavaScript is made easy with tools like **Webpacker** and **Import Maps**.

By the end of this chapter, you will:
Learn how to connect **Rails with Bootstrap, Tailwind, and Vue.js**.
Understand **asset management** with **Webpacker** and **Import Maps**.
Handle **forms, JavaScript**, and **AJAX requests** in Rails.

11.1 Connecting Rails with Bootstrap, Tailwind, and Vue.js

1. Connecting Rails with Bootstrap

Bootstrap is a popular CSS framework that makes front-end development faster and easier. It provides pre-designed components like navigation bars, buttons, forms, and modals.

Step 1: Install Bootstrap

If you're using **Rails 6** or later, you can install Bootstrap with **Webpacker**.

Add **Bootstrap** to your `Gemfile`:

```ruby

gem 'bootstrap', '~> 5.0'
```

Then, run:

```sh

bundle install
```

Install Bootstrap via Webpacker by adding it to the `application.js` **and** `application.scss` **files.**

Step 2: Add Bootstrap to Your JavaScript

In `app/javascript/packs/application.js`, **import Bootstrap:**

javascript

```
import "bootstrap"
```

Step 3: Add Bootstrap to Your Stylesheets

In `app/assets/stylesheets/application.scss`, import **Bootstrap:**

scss

```
@import 'bootstrap';
```

Now, you can use Bootstrap classes in your views:

html

```
<div class="container">
  <button class="btn btn-primary">Click Me</button>
</div>
```

141

This will give you a **responsive layout** with pre-designed buttons, forms, and grid systems.

---

2. Connecting Rails with Tailwind CSS

Tailwind CSS is a utility-first CSS framework that allows you to build custom designs quickly. It gives you more flexibility compared to traditional frameworks like Bootstrap.

Step 1: Install Tailwind CSS

To install **Tailwind CSS**, run:

```sh

rails new myapp --webpack=react
cd myapp
```

Then, add Tailwind to your `Gemfile`:

```ruby

gem 'tailwindcss-rails'
```

Run the installation command:

```sh
sh
```

```sh
bin/rails tailwindcss:install
```

This will configure Tailwind to your Rails project, including creating a default `tailwind.config.js` file.

Step 2: Add Tailwind Classes to Views

Now you can start using Tailwind classes directly in your views:

```html
html
```

```html
<div class="p-4 bg-blue-500 text-white rounded-lg">
  Hello, this is a Tailwind button!
</div>
```

Tailwind provides **utility classes** for margins, padding, colors, borders, etc., giving you full control over your layout and design without writing custom CSS.

---

3. Connecting Rails with Vue.js

Vue.js is a popular JavaScript framework for building reactive and interactive user interfaces.

Step 1: Install Vue.js with Webpacker

To install **Vue.js**, run the following command:

sh

```
rails webpacker:install:vue
```

This will install Vue.js and add the necessary configuration files to your Rails project.

Step 2: Create a Vue Component

Create a Vue component in app/javascript/components/hello.vue:

html

```
<template>
  <div>
    <h1>{{ message }}</h1>
    <button @click="changeMessage">Change Message</button>
  </div>
</template>
```

```
<script>
export default {
  data() {
    return {
      message: "Hello, Vue.js!"
    };
  },
  methods: {
    changeMessage() {
      this.message = "You clicked the button!";
    }
  }
};
</script>
```

Step 3: Use Vue Component in a Rails View

In your Rails view (`app/views/home/index.html.erb`), use Vue as follows:

erb

```
<div id="app"></div>
```

```erb
<%= javascript_pack_tag 'application' %>
```

In `app/javascript/packs/application.js`, import and mount the Vue component:

javascript

```
import Vue from 'vue'
import Hello from '../components/hello.vue'

document.addEventListener('DOMContentLoaded', ()
=> {
  new Vue({
    render: h => h(Hello)
  }).$mount('#app')
})
```

Now, you can interact with **Vue.js components** inside your Rails application!

11.2 Managing Assets with Webpacker and Import Maps

1. Asset Management with Webpacker

Webpacker is the default tool in Rails for handling JavaScript, CSS, and other assets. It provides integration with modern JavaScript tools like **React**, **Vue.js**, and **TypeScript**.

Using Webpacker for JavaScript

- Add JavaScript dependencies to your `package.json`.
- Use `import` statements to include third-party libraries in your JavaScript files.
- Webpacker compiles JavaScript and assets into optimized packages for production.

Example: To use **lodash** in your project, run:

```sh

yarn add lodash
```

Then, import it in your JavaScript file:

```javascript

import _ from 'lodash';

console.log(_.join(['Hello', 'World'], ' '));
```

Managing CSS with Webpacker

For styles, you can import **CSS** or **SASS/SCSS** files directly in JavaScript files:

```javascript

import '../stylesheets/application.css';
```

2. Asset Management with Import Maps

Starting from Rails 7, **Import Maps** are used as a simpler alternative to Webpacker for managing JavaScript assets without the need for Node.js or Yarn.

Step 1: Install Import Maps

Rails will install **Import Maps** for you by default in new applications. However, if you're adding it manually:

```sh
```

```sh
bin/rails importmap:install
```

Step 2: Adding JavaScript Libraries

You can add libraries without using Yarn or NPM. To add a library, modify `config/importmap.rb`:

```ruby
```

```ruby
pin "application", preload: true
pin "react", to: "https://cdn.skypack.dev/react"
pin            "react-dom",           to:
"https://cdn.skypack.dev/react-dom"
```

Now, in your JavaScript files, you can import libraries directly:

```
javascript
```

```
import React from "react"
import ReactDOM from "react-dom"
```

Import Maps are an excellent choice for small apps that don't require complex JavaScript tooling.

11.3 Handling Forms, JavaScript, and AJAX Requests

1. Handling Forms in Rails

Rails makes it easy to create forms using `form_with` helper methods.

Basic Form Example:

```erb
<%= form_with(model: @user, local: true) do |form| %>
  <%= form.label :name %>
  <%= form.text_field :name %>

  <%= form.label :email %>
```

149

```
  <%= form.email_field :email %>

  <%= form.submit "Submit" %>
<% end %>
```

This generates a form with the required fields. When the form is submitted, it will send data to the corresponding controller's `create` or `update` actions.

---

2. Handling JavaScript and AJAX Requests

To make dynamic requests, Rails provides **AJAX** functionality using **UJS (Unobtrusive JavaScript).**

Basic AJAX Example:

```
erb
```

```
<%= button_to 'Load More', posts_path, remote:
true, id: 'load-more' %>
```

In the controller, respond to AJAX requests:

```
ruby
```

```
def index
  @posts = Post.all
  respond_to do |format|
```

```
    format.html
    format.js
  end
end
```

Create `app/views/posts/index.js.erb`:

```
javascript
```

```
$('#posts').append('<%= j(render @posts) %>');
```

This allows the page to update dynamically without reloading the entire page.

Chapter Summary

Bootstrap, Tailwind, and Vue.js can be integrated with Rails to enhance the user interface. **Webpacker** and **Import Maps** help manage JavaScript and CSS assets efficiently. **Rails provides powerful helpers** for managing forms, JavaScript, and AJAX requests, enabling rich and interactive user experiences.

In the next chapter, we'll dive into **testing in Rails**, covering unit tests, integration tests, and best practices for ensuring a reliable application.

Next Chapter → Testing in Rails

CHAPTER 12

BUILDING INTERACTIVE FEATURES WITH TURBO AND STIMULUS

Introduction

Rails 7 introduced a powerful set of tools called **Hotwire**, which helps build **fast, interactive, and real-time features** without relying on heavy JavaScript frameworks. Hotwire combines **Turbo** for navigation and updates, and **Stimulus** for adding interactivity to your HTML.

By the end of this chapter, you will:
Understand **Hotwire** and how it simplifies building real-time, interactive apps.
Learn to use **Turbo Frames** and **Turbo Streams** for fast updates and navigation.
Integrate **Stimulus.js** to create dynamic user interactions with minimal JavaScript.

What is Hotwire?

Hotwire is a combination of **Turbo** and **Stimulus**, designed to reduce the complexity of building real-time web applications. It provides:

- **Turbo** for **page updates and navigation** (without full page reloads).
- **Stimulus** for **adding interactivity** to your views with minimal JavaScript.

Why Use Hotwire?

Hotwire helps you:

- Build **real-time updates** with minimal JavaScript.
- Avoid the complexity of managing client-side frameworks like React or Vue.
- Keep your app **fast and responsive** by sending HTML instead of JSON or JavaScript.

1. Turbo Frames – Speeding Up Navigation

Turbo Frames are a key part of **Turbo,** and they allow you to update portions of your page **without refreshing the entire page**. This means faster and more responsive user interactions.

Step 1: Adding Turbo to Your Application

If you're using Rails 7, **Turbo** is already included by default. Otherwise, you can install it via:

```sh

gem 'turbo-rails'
```

Then, run:

```sh

bundle install
```

Step 2: Using Turbo Frames

Turbo Frames allow you to update parts of your page without reloading the entire page. For example, let's create a partial that updates a list of comments.

In `app/views/posts/show.html.erb`, wrap the comments section in a `turbo-frame` tag:

155

erb

```erb
<h1><%= @post.title %></h1>

<turbo-frame id="comments">
  <%= render @post.comments %>
</turbo-frame>

<%=           form_with(model:        [@post,
@post.comments.build], local: false) do |form| %>
  <%= form.text_area :body %>
  <%= form.submit "Add Comment" %>
<% end %>
```

Here, the `id="comments"` ensures that only the comments section will be updated, and the page won't reload when a new comment is submitted.

Step 3: Handling Turbo Frame Updates

Create a partial for rendering comments in `app/views/comments/_comment.html.erb`:

erb

```erb
<p><%= comment.body %></p>
```

When a new comment is added, **Turbo** will update the section without a full-page reload.

156

2. Turbo Streams – Real-Time Updates

Turbo Streams enable **real-time updates** by automatically pushing changes to the page. This is great for features like live notifications, chat messages, or any content that updates frequently.

Step 1: Add Turbo Stream to Your Controller

Let's add real-time updates to comments.

In `app/controllers/comments_controller.rb`, modify the `create` action:

ruby

```ruby
def create
  @post = Post.find(params[:post_id])
  @comment                                =
@post.comments.build(comment_params)

  if @comment.save
    respond_to do |format|
      format.html { redirect_to @post, notice:
'Comment was successfully created.' }
      format.turbo_stream
```

```
      end
    else
      render :new
    end
end
```

Step 2: Create Turbo Stream Views

Create a Turbo Stream response in `app/views/comments/create.turbo_stream.erb`:

erb

```
<turbo-stream target="comments" action="append">
  <turbo-frame id="comment_<%= @comment.id %>">
    <%= render @comment %>
  </turbo-frame>
</turbo-stream>
```

When a new comment is added, it will automatically **appear in the comments section** in real-time without reloading the page.

12.3 Adding Dynamic Interactions with Stimulus.js

What is Stimulus?

Stimulus is a **JavaScript framework** that adds **interactivity** to HTML without requiring complex JavaScript code. It works seamlessly with Turbo, enabling you to enhance your pages with features like toggling visibility, form validation, or responding to user actions.

Step 1: Install Stimulus

If you're using Rails 7, Stimulus is also included by default. To install it in older versions, run:

```sh
rails webpacker:install:stimulus
```

Step 2: Creating a Stimulus Controller

Let's create a simple controller that shows or hides a message when a button is clicked.

Run:

```sh
rails generate stimulus toggle_message
```

This will create a Stimulus controller in `app/javascript/controllers/toggle_message_contr oller.js`:

```
javascript

import { Controller } from "stimulus";

export default class extends Controller {
  static targets = ["message"];

  toggle() {

this.messageTarget.classList.toggle("hidden");
  }
}
```

Step 3: Using the Stimulus Controller in Views

In `app/views/posts/show.html.erb`, add a button to toggle the visibility of a message:

```erb
<turbo-frame id="post_<%= @post.id %>">
  <h1><%= @post.title %></h1>

  <button            data-action="click->toggle-
message#toggle">Toggle Message</button>

  <div     data-toggle-message-target="message"
class="hidden">
    <p>This  message  can  be  toggled  on  and
off.</p>
```

```
</div>
</turbo-frame>
```

Here, the button triggers the `toggle` method in the `ToggleMessageController`, which shows or hides the message by adding or removing the `hidden` class.

Step 4: Adding More Dynamic Features

You can use Stimulus to add more dynamic behavior to your application. For example, creating a **live search** feature or **form validation** without needing to reload the page.

Live Search with Stimulus:

```javascript
import { Controller } from "stimulus";

export default class extends Controller {
  static targets = ["input", "results"];

  search() {
    let query = this.inputTarget.value;
    // Call an API or search method to get results
    this.resultsTarget.innerHTML = "Searching
for " + query;
```

```
  }
}
```

In the view:

erb

```
<input data-action="input->search#search" data-
search-target="input" placeholder="Search...">
<div data-search-target="results"></div>
```

This creates a **real-time search** feature that updates the results dynamically.

Chapter Summary

Turbo Frames and **Turbo Streams** enable **fast updates and real-time changes** to your views. **Stimulus.js** helps add **dynamic interactivity** to your pages with minimal JavaScript. **Hotwire** combines Turbo and Stimulus to **create reactive, real-time features** efficiently in Rails without the need for a heavy front-end framework.

In the next chapter, we'll cover **authentication and authorization in Rails**, including setting up secure user logins.

Next Chapter → Authentication and Authorization in Rails

CHAPTER 13

USER AUTHENTICATION WITH DEVISE AND OMNIAUTH

Introduction

User authentication and security are essential aspects of any web application. **Devise** and **OmniAuth** are two powerful gems in Rails for handling authentication and integrating third-party logins (e.g., Google, GitHub, Facebook). Devise provides a comprehensive solution for handling user authentication, while OmniAuth allows you to authenticate users using their social media accounts.

By the end of this chapter, you will: Learn how to set up **Devise** for user authentication in Rails. Implement **OAuth** authentication with **Google**, **GitHub**, and **Facebook** using **OmniAuth**. Implement **role-based access control** to manage user permissions.

13.1 Setting Up Devise for User Authentication

What is Devise?

Devise is a flexible and feature-rich authentication solution for Rails. It handles user registration, login, password recovery, and session management, and it supports various authentication strategies like email/password authentication, OAuth, and more.

Step 1: Install Devise

Add **Devise** to your `Gemfile`:

```ruby

gem 'devise'
```

Run the following command to install it:

```sh

bundle install
```

Then, run the generator to install Devise:

```sh
```

```
rails generate devise:install
```

This will create the necessary configuration files for Devise.

Step 2: Set Up the User Model

Create a `User` model with Devise:

```sh
```

```
rails generate devise User
```

This will create:

- A migration file for the `users` table.
- A `User` model in `app/models/user.rb`.

Step 3: Run the Migration

Run the migration to create the users table:

```sh
```

```
rails db:migrate
```

Step 4: Set Up Routes

Devise automatically adds routes for user authentication (login, logout, sign up, etc.) to your `config/routes.rb`. Make sure it includes the following:

166

```ruby
```

```ruby
devise_for :users
```

Step 5: Add Authentication Links

In your `app/views/layouts/application.html.erb`, add links to handle user login/logout:

```erb
```

```erb
<% if user_signed_in? %>
  <%=             link_to              'Logout',
destroy_user_session_path, method: :delete %>
<% else %>
  <%= link_to 'Login', new_user_session_path %>
|
  <%=           link_to           'Sign         Up',
new_user_registration_path %>
<% end %>
```

Step 6: Protect Pages with Authentication

To ensure that only logged-in users can access certain pages, use the `before_action` in your controllers. For example, to restrict access to the `dashboard` page:

```ruby
```

```
class          DashboardController          <
ApplicationController
  before_action :authenticate_user!

  def show
    # Your logic here
  end
end
```

Now, users must be signed in to access the dashboard.

13.2 Implementing OAuth with Google, GitHub, and Facebook

What is OAuth?

OAuth is a secure and widely used authentication protocol that allows users to authenticate with third-party services (like **Google**, **GitHub**, and **Facebook**) instead of using traditional email/password login.

Step 1: Install OmniAuth and OAuth Providers

Add **OmniAuth** and the required OAuth gems to your Gemfile:

```
ruby
```

```ruby
gem 'omniauth'
gem 'omniauth-google-oauth2'
gem 'omniauth-github'
gem 'omniauth-facebook'
```

Run:

```
sh
```

```sh
bundle install
```

Step 2: Configure OmniAuth

Create a new file in `config/initializers/omniauth.rb` to configure OmniAuth with your provider keys:

```
ruby
```

```ruby
Rails.application.config.middleware.use
OmniAuth::Builder do
  provider  :google_oauth2,  'GOOGLE_CLIENT_ID',
'GOOGLE_CLIENT_SECRET'
  provider      :github,      'GITHUB_CLIENT_ID',
'GITHUB_CLIENT_SECRET'
  provider      :facebook,     'FACEBOOK_APP_ID',
'FACEBOOK_APP_SECRET'
end
```

169

To get your keys:

- **Google:** Create a project on Google Developers Console and enable OAuth.
- **GitHub:** Create an OAuth application on GitHub.
- **Facebook:** Create an app on Facebook for Developers.

Step 3: Add OAuth Callbacks to the User Model

Modify the `User` model to handle OAuth authentication. In `app/models/user.rb`, add:

ruby

```
class User < ApplicationRecord
  devise    :omniauthable,    omniauth_providers:
[:google_oauth2, :github, :facebook]

  def self.from_omniauth(auth)
    user          =          User.where(email:
auth.info.email).first_or_initialize
    user.name = auth.info.name
    user.provider = auth.provider
    user.uid = auth.uid
    user.save
    user
  end
end
```

170

Here, the `from_omniauth` method creates a user or updates an existing one based on the OAuth provider's data.

Step 4: Handle OAuth Callbacks

Create a controller to handle the OAuth callbacks, such as `app/controllers/omniauth_callbacks_controller.rb`:

ruby

```ruby
class        OmniauthCallbacksController        <
ApplicationController
  def google_oauth2
    @user                                       =
User.from_omniauth(request.env["omniauth.auth"]
)
    sign_in_and_redirect @user, notice: "Signed
in successfully with Google."
  end

  def github
    @user                                       =
User.from_omniauth(request.env["omniauth.auth"]
)
    sign_in_and_redirect @user, notice: "Signed
in successfully with GitHub."
  end
```

```ruby
  def facebook
    @user                              =
User.from_omniauth(request.env["omniauth.auth"]
)
    sign_in_and_redirect @user, notice: "Signed
in successfully with Facebook."
  end
end
```

Step 5: Update Routes

Modify `config/routes.rb` to handle OAuth callbacks:

ruby

```ruby
devise_for      :users,        controllers:      {
omniauth_callbacks: 'omniauth_callbacks' }
```

Step 6: Add OAuth Links to the View

In your views, you can now add buttons to allow users to sign in via Google, GitHub, or Facebook:

erb

```erb
<%=  link_to   "Sign   in   with   Google",
user_google_oauth2_omniauth_authorize_path %>
<%=  link_to   "Sign   in   with   GitHub",
user_github_omniauth_authorize_path %>
```

```
<%= link_to "Sign in with Facebook",
user_facebook_omniauth_authorize_path %>
```

13.3 Role-Based Access Control

What is Role-Based Access Control?

Role-based access control (RBAC) allows you to restrict access to certain parts of your application based on the user's role. Common roles include **admin**, **user**, or **moderator**.

Step 1: Add a Role to the User Model

Generate a migration to add a `role` column to the `users` table:

sh

```
rails generate migration AddRoleToUsers
role:string
rails db:migrate
```

In `app/models/user.rb`, define default roles:

ruby

```
class User < ApplicationRecord
  enum role: { user: 0, admin: 1 }
```

173

```
# Other devise methods
end
```

Step 2: Assign Roles to Users

You can assign roles to users either through the Rails console or by setting a default in the user creation process.

In the Rails console:

```ruby
```

```ruby
user = User.create(name: "Admin User", email:
"admin@example.com", password: "password", role:
:admin)
```

Step 3: Restrict Access Based on Role

In your controllers, use `before_action` to restrict access to specific actions:

```ruby
```

```ruby
class AdminController < ApplicationController
  before_action :authenticate_user!
  before_action :check_admin_role

  def index
```

```
    # Admin-only content
  end


  private


  def check_admin_role
    redirect_to root_path, alert: "You are not
authorized  to  access  this  page."  unless
current_user.admin?
  end
end
```

Here, only users with the `admin` role can access the `AdminController`.

Chapter Summary

Devise provides a comprehensive solution for **user authentication**.

OmniAuth integrates third-party OAuth logins (Google, GitHub, Facebook).

Role-based access control ensures that only authorized users can access certain resources.

In the next chapter, we'll explore **advanced security features** like **password encryption**, **CSRF protection**, and **securing sensitive data**.

Next Chapter → Advanced Security Features in Rails

CHAPTER 14

SECURING RAILS APPLICATIONS

Introduction

Security is a crucial aspect of web development, and Rails provides a variety of tools and practices to ensure that your application is protected against common vulnerabilities. In this chapter, we will cover the best practices for securing Rails applications, including protection against **SQL injection**, **Cross-Site Scripting (XSS)**, and **Cross-Site Request Forgery (CSRF)**. We'll also discuss how to implement **secure password storage** and follow **best security practices**.

By the end of this chapter, you will:
Learn how to protect against **SQL injection**, **XSS**, and **CSRF** attacks.
Understand how to **securely store passwords** using hashing.
Implement **best security practices** to make your Rails application more secure.

177

14.1 Protecting Against SQL Injection, XSS, and CSRF

1. Protecting Against SQL Injection

SQL injection is an attack where malicious SQL queries are injected into an application's input fields to manipulate the database. To protect against SQL injection, Rails provides **ActiveRecord** and **prepared statements** that automatically sanitize user inputs.

How Rails Prevents SQL Injection:

When you use **ActiveRecord** queries, Rails automatically escapes user input, preventing malicious SQL from being executed.

Example of SQL Injection:

Without protection, if user input is inserted directly into SQL queries, it can lead to SQL injection:

```ruby
ruby

User.where("email  =  '#{params[:email]}'  AND
password = '#{params[:password]}'")
```

An attacker could input:

```
text
```

```
email = "admin@example.com' OR '1'='1"
```

This would turn the query into:

```
sql
```

```
SELECT  *  FROM  users  WHERE  email  =
'admin@example.com' OR '1'='1' AND password = ''
```

To prevent this, **ActiveRecord** uses **prepared statements**:

```
ruby
```

```
User.where(email:   params[:email],   password:
params[:password])
```

This ensures that user input is treated as data, not executable code, thus preventing SQL injection.

2. Protecting Against XSS (Cross-Site Scripting)

XSS attacks occur when an attacker injects malicious scripts into a web application, which then execute in the browser of users visiting the page. Rails automatically escapes HTML by default, protecting against XSS.

How Rails Prevents XSS:

Rails escapes all user-generated content by default using the `html_escape` method, so input like:

ruby

```
params[:name]                                    =
"<script>alert('Hacked!')</script>"
```

will be automatically converted to:

html

```
&lt;script&gt;alert('Hacked!')&lt;/script&gt;
```

To safely display user input, use `<%= %>`:

erb

```
<p><%= @user.name %></p>
```

This ensures that any potentially dangerous HTML or JavaScript is **escaped** and doesn't execute in the user's browser.

Unescaped Output (Only when Necessary):

In rare cases, when you are sure the content is safe (e.g., sanitized HTML), you can use `raw` to prevent escaping:

erb

```
<%= raw @user.bio %>
```

But be cautious—only use `raw` when you're confident the content is secure.

3. Protecting Against CSRF (Cross-Site Request Forgery)

CSRF is an attack where a malicious user is tricked into performing actions on behalf of an authenticated user without their consent. Rails provides **built-in protection** against CSRF attacks by using **authenticity tokens**.

How Rails Protects Against CSRF:

- Rails includes an **authenticity token** in forms to ensure the request is coming from your application.
- If the authenticity token doesn't match the expected value, Rails will reject the request.

Rails automatically includes the CSRF token in all forms by using the `form_with` helper:

erb

```erb
<%= form_with(model: @user) do |form| %>
  <%= form.text_field :name %>
  <%= form.submit "Submit" %>
<% end %>
```

This generates an `<input>` field for the CSRF token, ensuring that the request is valid. You don't need to manually manage CSRF protection unless you are making external API requests.

14.2 Implementing Secure Password Storage

1. Using BCrypt for Secure Password Hashing

Never store passwords in plain text. Instead, store a **hashed version** of the password using a secure algorithm like **BCrypt**. Rails comes with **Devise**, which uses BCrypt by default for password hashing.

How BCrypt Works:

BCrypt is a secure hashing algorithm that adds a **salt** (random data) to the password before hashing it, making it resistant to rainbow table attacks.

Setting Up BCrypt in Rails:

Devise automatically handles password hashing using BCrypt. However, if you're implementing authentication manually, you can use the **BCrypt** gem:

Add it to your Gemfile:

```ruby
```

```ruby
gem 'bcrypt', '~> 3.1.7'
```

Run:

```sh
```

```sh
bundle install
```

Storing and Verifying Passwords:

In your User model, store the password as follows:

```ruby
```

```ruby
class User < ApplicationRecord
  has_secure_password
end
```

`has_secure_password` automatically handles:

- **Password hashing** with BCrypt.
- **Password confirmation** for user validation.

When a user signs up, you can create a user with:

ruby

```ruby
user = User.create(name: "Alice", email: "alice@example.com", password: "securepassword")
```

When authenticating, compare the entered password to the hashed password stored in the database:

ruby

```ruby
user.authenticate("securepassword")  # Returns user if the password is correct, false if incorrect.
```

This ensures that passwords are **never stored in plain text** and are protected by strong hashing.

14.3 Best Security Practices for Rails Applications

1. Enable HTTPS (SSL/TLS)

Always use **HTTPS** to secure data in transit between the client and the server. Rails provides a simple way to force HTTPS by enabling the `force_ssl` option.

In `config/application.rb`, add:

```ruby
```

```
config.force_ssl = true
```

This ensures all traffic is encrypted using SSL/TLS.

2. Use Strong Passwords

Ensure that your application enforces strong passwords. Devise already provides password strength validation, but you can customize the password policy further. For example, you can enforce a **minimum length** or require **special characters**:

```ruby
```

```
validates :password, length: { minimum: 8 }
```

You can also use additional gems like **devise-security** to enforce stronger password policies.

3. Limit Login Attempts

To prevent brute-force attacks, limit the number of **failed login attempts**. Devise has a built-in feature called **lockable** that locks an account after a set number of failed attempts.

Enable this feature in your `User` model:

ruby

```
devise          :lockable,          lock_strategy:
:failed_attempts, unlock_strategy: :email
```

This will lock the user's account after a certain number of failed login attempts and send an email to the user to unlock it.

4. Implement Two-Factor Authentication (2FA)

Two-Factor Authentication (2FA) adds an extra layer of security by requiring users to verify their identity using a second factor (e.g., a code sent via SMS or an authentication app). Devise integrates with **two-factor authentication** gems like **devise-two-factor**.

Add it to your Gemfile:

```ruby
gem 'devise-two-factor'
```

Run:

```sh
bundle install
```

Configure Devise to enable 2FA in your application.

5. Keep Dependencies Up to Date

Regularly update your gems and Rails version to ensure that your app stays secure and free from known vulnerabilities. Use tools like **Bundler Audit** to check for security issues in your dependencies.

```sh
gem install bundler-audit
bundler-audit check
```

6. Use Security Headers

To protect your application from certain types of attacks, ensure that you use proper **security headers** such as X-Content-Type-Options, Strict-Transport-Security, and Content-Security-Policy.

Rails provides an easy way to configure security headers using the secure_headers **gem:**

```ruby
ruby
```

```ruby
gem 'secure_headers'
```

Run:

```sh
sh
```

```sh
bundle install
```

Then configure it in an initializer to enable headers like X-Frame-Options, X-Content-Type-Options, and others.

Chapter Summary

Rails provides built-in protections against SQL injection, XSS, and CSRF attacks. **Devise** automatically handles **secure password storage** using **BCrypt** for hashing. **Best security practices** for Rails applications include using HTTPS, limiting login attempts, enforcing strong passwords, and regularly updating dependencies.

In the next chapter, we'll dive into **performance optimization techniques** for Rails applications to keep your app fast and scalable.

Next Chapter → Performance Optimization in Rails

CHAPTER 15

BACKGROUND JOBS AND ASYNCHRONOUS PROCESSING

Introduction

Handling long-running tasks such as sending emails, processing payments, or generating reports can significantly slow down the user experience if processed synchronously (i.e., directly within the web request cycle). To solve this, Rails provides tools for **background job processing**, which allows you to run tasks **asynchronously** without blocking the user's interaction with the application.

In this chapter, we will cover how to: Use **Active Job** with background job frameworks like **Sidekiq** and **Resque**. Efficiently **process background tasks** in Rails. **Schedule jobs** using **Cron** and the **Whenever gem**.

15.1 Using Active Job with Sidekiq and Resque

What is Active Job?

190

Active Job is a framework in Rails that allows you to run background tasks. It provides a common interface for different queueing backends (e.g., Sidekiq, Resque, and Delayed Job), so you can easily swap out backends without changing the rest of your application code.

By default, Rails uses **async** for background jobs in development, but for production apps, we usually want a more robust solution like **Sidekiq** or **Resque**.

---

1. Setting Up Sidekiq for Background Jobs

Sidekiq is a powerful and efficient background job processing library that uses threads to handle multiple jobs concurrently, making it ideal for high-volume applications.

Step 1: Add Sidekiq to Your Gemfile

Add **Sidekiq** to your `Gemfile`:

```ruby
```

```
gem 'sidekiq'
```

Then, run:

```sh
```

```
bundle install
```

Step 2: Configure Sidekiq in Rails

Create an initializer to configure **Sidekiq**. In `config/initializers/sidekiq.rb`, add:

```ruby
```

```
Sidekiq.configure_server do |config|
  config.redis        =        { url:
'redis://localhost:6379/0' }
end

Sidekiq.configure_client do |config|
  config.redis        =        { url:
'redis://localhost:6379/0' }
end
```

Ensure you have **Redis** running on your local machine or use a Redis cloud provider. Redis is required for Sidekiq to manage the job queue.

Step 3: Create a Job

Use Rails' `ActiveJob` API to define background jobs. For example, let's create a job to send an email:

sh

```
rails generate job SendEmail
```

This generates a file in `app/jobs/send_email_job.rb`:

ruby

```ruby
class SendEmailJob < ApplicationJob
  queue_as :default

  def perform(user)
    # Code to send email
    UserMailer.welcome_email(user).deliver_now
  end
end
```

Step 4: Enqueue a Job

You can now enqueue jobs to be processed by Sidekiq. For example, in a controller or model:

ruby

```ruby
SendEmailJob.perform_later(@user)
```

This will add the job to the queue, and Sidekiq will process it asynchronously in the background.

Step 5: Start Sidekiq

To start processing jobs with Sidekiq, run:

```sh

bundle exec sidekiq
```

You can now view job processing logs and check job statuses in the Sidekiq web interface.

2. Setting Up Resque for Background Jobs

Resque is another popular background job library that uses Redis for job queue management. It's simpler than Sidekiq but still effective for background processing.

Step 1: Add Resque to Your Gemfile

```ruby

gem 'resque'
```

Run:

```sh

bundle install
```

Step 2: Configure Resque

In `config/initializers/resque.rb`, **configure Resque:**

ruby

```
Resque.redis               =               Redis.new(url:
'redis://localhost:6379/0')
```

Step 3: Create a Job

Create a job class to define your background task:

ruby

```
class SendEmailJob
  @queue = :email_queue

  def self.perform(user_id)
    user = User.find(user_id)
    UserMailer.welcome_email(user).deliver_now
  end
end
```

Step 4: Enqueue a Job

To enqueue the job, you would use:

ruby

```
Resque.enqueue(SendEmailJob, @user.id)
```

195

Step 5: Start Resque Worker

To process jobs, run a worker process:

```sh

QUEUE=email_queue rake resque:work
```

This will start processing jobs from the `email_queue` in Resque.

15.2 Processing Background Tasks Efficiently

Handling Job Failures

Both **Sidekiq** and **Resque** allow you to handle job failures. For example, in **Sidekiq**, you can define a `retry` policy and add custom error handling.

```ruby

class SendEmailJob < ApplicationJob
  queue_as :default

  retry_on   StandardError,   wait:   5.seconds,
attempts: 3
```

```
def perform(user)
  UserMailer.welcome_email(user).deliver_now
end
end
```

This will retry the job **3 times** if it raises an exception, with a **5-second delay** between attempts.

In **Resque**, you can handle failures by using the `failure` mechanism, and you can even define your own **failure backend** to log errors or notify administrators.

Monitoring Jobs

- **Sidekiq**: Provides a built-in web interface for monitoring jobs. To enable it, add this to your `config/routes.rb`:

  ruby

  ```ruby
  require 'sidekiq/web'
  mount Sidekiq::Web => '/sidekiq'
  ```

- **Resque**: Use the `resque-web` gem to monitor jobs in a web interface:

  ruby

```
gem 'resque-web'
```

Add this to your `config/routes.rb`:

```ruby
```

```
require 'resque/server'
mount Resque::Server.new, at: '/resque'
```

15.3 Scheduling Jobs with Cron and Whenever

1. Scheduling Jobs with Cron

Cron is a time-based job scheduler in Unix-like operating systems. You can use it to run jobs at specific intervals, such as hourly, daily, or weekly.

Rails doesn't natively provide Cron job management, but you can use **Whenever**, a gem that simplifies the process.

Step 1: Install Whenever Gem

Add **Whenever** to your `Gemfile`:

```ruby
```

```
gem 'whenever', require: false
```

Run:

```sh
```

```sh
bundle install
```

Step 2: Define Cron Jobs

Generate the `schedule.rb` file:

```sh
```

```sh
wheneverize .
```

This creates a `config/schedule.rb` file, where you can define your jobs. For example:

```ruby
```

```ruby
every 1.day, at: '4:30 am' do
  runner "User.send_daily_reports"
end
```

This will run the `send_daily_reports` method of the `User` model every day at 4:30 AM.

Step 3: Update Crontab

Run this command to update the system's crontab with the defined schedule:

```sh

```

```
whenever --update-crontab
```

Now, your job will be automatically scheduled and executed by Cron.

---

2. Scheduling Jobs with Sidekiq Cron

If you're using **Sidekiq**, you can also schedule jobs using **Sidekiq-Cron**.

Step 1: Install Sidekiq-Cron

Add to your `Gemfile`:

```ruby

```

```
gem 'sidekiq-cron'
```

Run:

```sh

```

```
bundle install
```

Step 2: Define Cron Jobs for Sidekiq

Create a cron job with Sidekiq-Cron:

```ruby

require 'sidekiq/cron/job'

Sidekiq::Cron::Job.create(
  name: 'Send daily reports',
  cron: '0 4 * * *',
  class: 'SendReportJob'
)
```

This will schedule the SendReportJob to run at **4 AM every day**.

Chapter Summary

Sidekiq and Resque are both excellent options for handling background jobs in Rails, with Sidekiq offering better performance due to multi-threading. **Active Job** provides a unified interface for background processing, making it easy to switch between different job backends. Use **Cron** or **Sidekiq-Cron** for scheduling tasks, and use

Whenever for simple Cron job management. Always consider **retry mechanisms** and **error handling** for background jobs to ensure reliability.

In the next chapter, we will dive into **performance optimization** strategies for your Rails applications to keep them fast and scalable.

Next Chapter → Performance Optimization in Rails

CHAPTER 16

CACHING STRATEGIES IN RAILS

Introduction

Caching is one of the most effective ways to improve the performance and scalability of your Rails applications. By storing frequently accessed data in memory, you can reduce database queries, lower response times, and decrease server load. In this chapter, we will explore different caching strategies such as **page**, **fragment**, and **low-level caching**. We will also discuss how to use **Redis** for caching and performance boosts, as well as how to implement **CDN caching strategies** for even better global performance.

By the end of this chapter, you will: Understand the different types of **caching** available in Rails. Learn how to use **Redis** for caching in Rails. Implement **CDN caching strategies** to improve content delivery speed and reduce server load.

15.1 Page, Fragment, and Low-Level Caching

1. Page Caching

Page caching is the simplest and most effective caching strategy for static content. It caches the entire HTML page and serves it directly from the cache, bypassing the Rails application entirely. This is ideal for content that doesn't change frequently, like static informational pages.

How Page Caching Works

Page caching stores the **entire response** for a given URL. The next time a user visits the same page, the cached HTML is served directly.

Setting Up Page Caching in Rails

Rails page caching can be enabled via the `caches_page` method in controllers.

For example, in `app/controllers/posts_controller.rb`:

```ruby
class PostsController < ApplicationController
```

```
caches_page :show

def show
  @post = Post.find(params[:id])
end
end
```

This caches the entire page when a post is viewed. The next time a request for the same post is made, the cached version of the page is served.

Limitations of Page Caching:

- Not suitable for pages with dynamic content.
- Requires manual invalidation if the content changes.

---

2. Fragment Caching

Fragment caching is more flexible than page caching and is useful when only parts of a page need to be cached. For example, you might cache a list of recent posts but not the user-specific comments section.

How Fragment Caching Works

With fragment caching, you cache specific sections of a page (called fragments), rather than the entire page.

Setting Up Fragment Caching in Rails

Use the `cache` helper in your views to cache specific sections.

For example, in `app/views/posts/show.html.erb`:

erb

```
<%= cache @post do %>
  <div class="post">
    <h1><%= @post.title %></h1>
    <p><%= @post.body %></p>
  </div>
<% end %>
```

This caches only the section inside the `cache` block. When the page is requested again, Rails will serve the cached version of the post's content.

You can also use **cache keys** to ensure that a fragment is invalidated when the underlying data changes:

206

erb

```
<%= cache([@post, @post.comments]) do %>
  <div class="comments">
    <%= render @post.comments %>
  </div>
<% end %>
```

This caches the comments for the specific post, and it will automatically invalidate the cache when the post or its comments are updated.

---

3. Low-Level Caching

Low-level caching allows you to store arbitrary data in the cache, giving you full control over what gets cached. You can cache things like database query results, API responses, or complex computations.

How Low-Level Caching Works

Low-level caching involves explicitly storing data in the cache and retrieving it when needed. This is useful for frequently accessed data that doesn't change often.

Setting Up Low-Level Caching in Rails

Rails provides a `Rails.cache` object for low-level caching. You can store and retrieve arbitrary data:

ruby

```
# Store data in the cache
Rails.cache.write("recent_posts", Post.recent)

# Retrieve data from the cache
recent_posts = Rails.cache.read("recent_posts")

# Check if the data is present
if Rails.cache.exist?("recent_posts")
  recent_posts                              =
Rails.cache.read("recent_posts")
else
  recent_posts = Post.recent
  Rails.cache.write("recent_posts",
recent_posts)
end
```

You can also set an expiration time for cached data:

ruby

```
Rails.cache.write("recent_posts",    Post.recent,
expires_in: 5.minutes)
```

Low-level caching is ideal for caching **complex queries** or data that's expensive to generate.

15.2 Using Redis for Caching and Performance Boosts

What is Redis?

Redis is an in-memory key-value store that can be used for caching. It is known for its speed and ability to handle large amounts of data. Redis is commonly used in Rails to store cached data and improve application performance.

Step 1: Install Redis

You can install Redis on your local machine or use a Redis cloud provider. To install Redis locally on **macOS**:

sh

```
brew install redis
```

On **Ubuntu**:

sh

```
sudo apt-get install redis-server
```

Once Redis is installed, start the Redis server:

sh

```
redis-server
```

Step 2: Configuring Rails to Use Redis for Caching

Add the **Redis** gem to your `Gemfile`:

ruby

```
gem 'redis'
```

Run:

sh

```
bundle install
```

Then, configure Rails to use Redis for caching by modifying `config/environments/production.rb`:

ruby

```
config.cache_store       =       :redis_store,
"redis://localhost:6379/0/cache",  {  expires_in:
90.minutes }
```

Now, Rails will use Redis as the caching backend, and cached data will be stored in Redis.

Step 3: Using Redis for Caching

You can now use Redis for caching in the same way as with the default caching store:

ruby

```
Rails.cache.write("recent_posts", Post.recent)
recent_posts = Rails.cache.read("recent_posts")
```

Since Redis is an in-memory store, it's extremely fast and efficient for read-heavy applications.

15.3 Implementing CDN Caching Strategies

What is a CDN (Content Delivery Network)?

A **CDN** is a network of servers that caches static assets (like images, JavaScript, CSS, and videos) and serves them to users from the server closest to them. This reduces latency and speeds up content delivery.

211

Popular CDNs include **Cloudflare, Amazon CloudFront,** and **Fastly**.

Step 1: Configure Rails to Use a CDN

To serve assets via a CDN in Rails, configure the `config.asset_host` in `config/environments/production.rb`:

```ruby
config.action_controller.asset_host = "https://your-cdn-url.com"
```

This tells Rails to use the CDN for serving assets like images, stylesheets, and JavaScript files.

Step 2: Set Cache-Control Headers for Assets

Use `Cache-Control` headers to ensure that assets are cached by the CDN. For example:

```ruby
config.public_file_server.headers = {
  'Cache-Control' => 'public, max-age=31536000'
}
```

This instructs the CDN to cache assets for **one year**. You can adjust the `max-age` to suit your needs.

Step 3: Cache Busting for Assets

To avoid serving stale assets when you update them, use **asset versioning** (Rails does this automatically). The asset file names will include a **digest** that changes whenever the file content changes, ensuring that the CDN serves the latest version.

For example, in the `application.css`:

css

```
/* application-abc123.css */
```

When you update the file, the digest will change, ensuring that the CDN serves the latest version.

Chapter Summary

Page, **fragment**, and **low-level caching** allow you to cache different parts of a Rails application for improved performance.

Redis is an excellent caching solution for high-speed, in-memory caching. Implementing **CDN caching strategies** helps serve static assets quickly and efficiently across the globe.

In the next chapter, we'll explore **performance optimization** techniques for backend services to make your Rails applications even faster and more scalable.

Next Chapter → Performance Optimization in Rails

CHAPTER 17

SEARCH AND FILTERING WITH ELASTICSEARCH AND RANSACK

Introduction

Searching and filtering data efficiently is crucial in many web applications. Rails provides several ways to implement search functionality, and two popular tools for this purpose are **Elasticsearch** and **Ransack**. **Elasticsearch** is a powerful, scalable search engine, ideal for full-text search across large datasets, while **Ransack** provides a simple and easy way to filter and search ActiveRecord objects.

By the end of this chapter, you will: Learn how to add **powerful search capabilities** to Rails apps with **Elasticsearch**. Implement **full-text search** with Elasticsearch for fast and relevant results. Use **Ransack** to implement **advanced filtering** in your Rails applications.

What is Elasticsearch?

Elasticsearch is a distributed search engine based on **Lucene**. It provides powerful full-text search capabilities and is scalable, making it an excellent choice for large applications that need efficient, fast searching.

Why Use Elasticsearch in Rails?

Elasticsearch allows you to:

- Perform **full-text search** across large datasets.
- Handle complex queries and filter results with **faceting**, **sorting**, and **aggregations**.
- Scale easily as the amount of data grows.

While Rails provides basic ActiveRecord queries, Elasticsearch is ideal when your app needs **advanced search capabilities**, such as **autocomplete**, **highlighting**, and **fuzzy search**.

Step 1: Installing Elasticsearch

To use Elasticsearch in your Rails application, you need to install and configure the Elasticsearch server and then integrate it into your app using a Ruby gem like **elasticsearch-rails**.

Install Elasticsearch on Your System

You can install Elasticsearch on your local machine or use a hosted Elasticsearch service.

For **macOS**, use Homebrew:

```sh

brew install elasticsearch
```

For **Ubuntu**, run:

```sh

sudo apt-get install elasticsearch
```

Start the Elasticsearch server:

```sh

elasticsearch
```

Ensure that Elasticsearch is running on `http://localhost:9200` (default).

Install the Elasticsearch Rails Gem

Add the `elasticsearch-rails` gem to your `Gemfile`:

```ruby
gem 'elasticsearch-rails'
gem 'elasticsearch-model'
```

Run:

```sh
bundle install
```

This will install the necessary dependencies for integrating Elasticsearch with your Rails app.

Step 2: Integrating Elasticsearch with Models

You can integrate Elasticsearch with any ActiveRecord model that you want to enable search functionality for. For example, let's integrate Elasticsearch into the `Post` model.

218

Add Search Functionality to the Post Model

In your `app/models/post.rb`, include the `Elasticsearch::Model` and `Elasticsearch::Model::Callbacks` modules to enable searching and callbacks:

ruby

```ruby
class Post < ApplicationRecord
  include Elasticsearch::Model
  include Elasticsearch::Model::Callbacks

  # Define any custom methods or mappings if
necessary
end
```

The `Elasticsearch::Model::Callbacks` module will automatically index records when they are created, updated, or deleted.

Step 3: Indexing Data

To create the index and populate it with data from your `Post` model, run:

sh

```
rails console
Post.import
```

This will import all existing records in the `posts` table into the Elasticsearch index.

Step 4: Searching with Elasticsearch

To search the `Post` model, use the `search` method provided by Elasticsearch:

ruby

```
Post.search("your search query")
```

For example, if you want to search for posts containing the word "Rails":

ruby

```
Post.search("Rails")
```

This will return all posts where the text of the post contains the word "Rails". You can customize the search by adding more complex queries, sorting, and filtering.

Step 5: Advanced Search Features

Elasticsearch supports advanced search features like **fuzzy matching**, **wildcards**, **boosting** specific fields, and more.

For example, to perform a **fuzzy search** for posts:

ruby

```
Post.search({ query: { fuzzy: { title: "rail" }
} })
```

This will return posts with titles that are similar to "rail", accounting for slight misspellings.

15.2 Implementing Full-Text Search with Elasticsearch

Full-Text Search Example

In Elasticsearch, you can use **full-text search** to find documents (records) that contain specific words or phrases, even if they are spread across different fields. Let's enhance the search functionality to work with multiple fields.

Step 1: Customizing the Elasticsearch Query

To create a more advanced query that searches both the `title` and `body` fields of posts, you can use a **multi-match query**:

ruby

```
Post.search({
  query: {
    multi_match: {
      query: "Rails tutorial",
      fields: ["title", "body"]
    }
  }
})
```

This query searches for posts that contain the phrase **"Rails tutorial"** in either the `title` or `body` fields.

Step 2: Using Filters and Aggregations

You can also filter the results based on certain criteria. For example, to only return posts created after a certain date, you can add a filter:

ruby

```
Post.search({
  query: {
    multi_match: {
      query: "Rails tutorial",
      fields: ["title", "body"]
    }
  },
  filter: {
    range: {
      created_at: { gte: "2021-01-01" }
    }
  }
})
```

This will only return posts that contain "Rails tutorial" and were created after **January 1, 2021**.

15.3 Using Ransack for Advanced Filtering

What is Ransack?

Ransack is a gem that provides **advanced search and filtering** capabilities for ActiveRecord models. It allows you to easily build dynamic search forms for your application without needing to write complex query logic.

Step 1: Install the Ransack Gem

Add **Ransack** to your `Gemfile`:

```ruby
ruby
```

```ruby
gem 'ransack'
```

Run:

```sh
sh
```

```sh
bundle install
```

Step 2: Implementing Ransack in Your Controller

In your controller (e.g., `PostsController`), use `ransack` to set up search functionality:

```ruby
ruby
```

```ruby
class PostsController < ApplicationController
  def index
    @q = Post.ransack(params[:q])
    @posts = @q.result(distinct: true)
  end
end
```

Here, `ransack` takes the search parameters (`params[:q]`) and applies them to the model. The `result` method returns the filtered results.

Step 3: Building the Search Form

In your view (`app/views/posts/index.html.erb`), create a form to search for posts:

erb

```erb
<%= search_form_for @q do |f| %>
  <%= f.label :title_cont, "Title" %>
  <%= f.text_field :title_cont %>

  <%= f.label :body_cont, "Body" %>
  <%= f.text_field :body_cont %>

  <%= f.submit "Search" %>
<% end %>
```

Here, `:title_cont` and `:body_cont` are Ransack predicates for **partial matching**. You can use various predicates like `:eq` for exact matches, `:lt` for less than, and many others.

Step 4: Filtering with Ransack

You can now filter posts by title and body. For example, if you want to search for posts with the word "Rails" in the title, you can use the form:

```
html
```

```
Title: "Rails"
Body: ""
```

This will return posts where the title contains "Rails".

Using Complex Filters with Ransack

Ransack allows you to create **complex filtering** using a combination of conditions. For example, you can create filters that use multiple fields, ranges, or even joins between models.

```ruby
ruby
```

```ruby
@q = Post.ransack(title_or_body_cont: "Rails",
created_at_gteq: Date.today)
@posts = @q.result(distinct: true)
```

This searches for posts that contain "Rails" in the title or body and were created today or later.

Chapter Summary

Elasticsearch provides a powerful and scalable solution for **full-text search** and complex filtering in Rails applications. **Ransack** makes it easy to add **advanced search and filtering** capabilities without complex query logic. Use **Elasticsearch** for large datasets with advanced search requirements, and **Ransack** for simpler, in-app filtering functionality.

In the next chapter, we'll explore **advanced testing strategies** in Rails, including testing background jobs, APIs, and integrating with external services.

Next Chapter → Advanced Testing in Rails

CHAPTER 18

TESTING RAILS APPLICATIONS

Introduction

Testing is a crucial part of the software development process, ensuring that your application behaves as expected and that changes to the codebase don't introduce new bugs. In this chapter, we will explore the essential testing strategies for Rails applications, including **unit tests**, **integration tests**, and **system tests**. We will also dive into using **RSpec** and **Capybara** for effective testing and explore the benefits of **Test-Driven Development (TDD)** in Rails.

By the end of this chapter, you will: Understand the differences between **unit**, **integration**, and **system** **tests** in Rails. Learn how to write tests using **RSpec** and **Capybara**. Implement **Test-Driven Development (TDD)** in your Rails applications to improve code quality.

18.1 Writing Unit, Integration, and System Tests

1. Unit Tests

Unit tests are designed to test individual methods or functions within a class. They are isolated tests that check if a specific piece of functionality works as intended.

In Rails, **unit tests** typically focus on **models**. These tests check if your business logic (methods, validations, etc.) behaves correctly.

Example of a Unit Test in Rails

Suppose you have a `User` model with a method `full_name`:

ruby

```ruby
class User < ApplicationRecord
  def full_name
    "#{first_name} #{last_name}"
  end
end
```

To test this method, you can write a unit test like this:

ruby

```
# test/models/user_test.rb
require 'test_helper'

class UserTest < ActiveSupport::TestCase
  test "full_name returns the correct name" do
    user   =   User.new(first_name:   "John",
last_name: "Doe")
    assert_equal "John Doe", user.full_name
  end
end
```

In this example, the test verifies that the `full_name` method correctly combines the `first_name` and `last_name`.

Writing Unit Tests in RSpec

In **RSpec**, unit tests can be written using `describe` and `it` blocks:

```
ruby
```

```
# spec/models/user_spec.rb
require 'rails_helper'

RSpec.describe User, type: :model do
  it "returns the correct full name" do
    user   =   User.new(first_name:   "John",
last_name: "Doe")
    expect(user.full_name).to eq("John Doe")
```

```
    end
end
```

---

2. Integration Tests

Integration tests verify the interaction between different parts of the application. These tests ensure that the models, controllers, and views work together as expected.

For example, you might test whether a `User` can sign up through a form and get redirected to a profile page.

Example of an Integration Test
ruby

```
# test/integration/user_signup_test.rb
require 'test_helper'

class              UserSignupTest              <
ActionDispatch::IntegrationTest
  test "user can sign up" do
    get signup_path
    assert_response :success
    post  users_path,  params:  {  user:  {
first_name:  "John",  last_name:  "Doe",  email:
"john@example.com", password: "password" } }
    follow_redirect!
```

```
    assert_response :success
    assert_select "h1", "Welcome, John Doe!"
  end
end
```

This test checks if a user can successfully sign up, be redirected, and see their name on the welcome page.

Writing Integration Tests in RSpec

In RSpec, integration tests are written using `feature` blocks to simulate user interactions.

ruby

```
# spec/features/user_signup_spec.rb
require 'rails_helper'

RSpec.feature "User Signups", type: :feature do
  scenario "user can sign up successfully" do
    visit signup_path
    fill_in "First Name", with: "John"
    fill_in "Last Name", with: "Doe"
    fill_in "Email", with: "john@example.com"
    fill_in "Password", with: "password"
    click_button "Sign Up"

    expect(page).to have_content("Welcome, John
Doe!")
```

```
  end
end
```

3. System Tests

System tests are end-to-end tests that simulate real user interactions with the web application. They run in a browser, just like an actual user would, and ensure that the entire system (including JavaScript interactions) works as expected.

Rails uses **Capybara** for system tests, which can simulate user actions like clicking buttons, filling in forms, and checking page content.

Example of a System Test in Rails

ruby

```
# test/system/user_signup_system_test.rb
require "application_system_test_case"

class          UserSignupSystemTest          <
ApplicationSystemTestCase
  test "user can sign up" do
    visit signup_path
    fill_in "First Name", with: "John"
    fill_in "Last Name", with: "Doe"
```

```
    fill_in "Email", with: "john@example.com"
    fill_in "Password", with: "password"
    click_on "Sign Up"
    assert_text "Welcome, John Doe!"
  end
end
```

This test interacts with the page and checks that the user is correctly signed up.

18.2 Using RSpec and Capybara for Testing

1. Setting Up RSpec

RSpec is a popular testing framework in the Ruby community that provides a more readable and flexible syntax for writing tests.

Step 1: Install RSpec

Add the **RSpec** gems to your `Gemfile`:

```ruby

gem 'rspec-rails'
gem 'capybara'
```

Run the following commands to install:

```sh
```

```
bundle install
rails generate rspec:install
```

This will set up the necessary configuration files for RSpec.

Step 2: Writing RSpec Tests

RSpec tests are written using `describe`, `context`, and `it` blocks:

```ruby
```

```ruby
RSpec.describe User, type: :model do
  it "returns the full name" do
    user   =   User.new(first_name:   "John",
last_name: "Doe")
    expect(user.full_name).to eq("John Doe")
  end
end
```

2. Setting Up Capybara

Capybara is used to simulate user interactions for system tests. It allows you to interact with the app just like a real user would (e.g., clicking buttons, filling forms).

Step 1: Install Capybara

Capybara is already included in the `Gemfile` when you add `rspec-rails`, but if it's not there, you can add it manually:

ruby

```ruby
gem 'capybara'
```

Then, run:

sh

```sh
bundle install
```

Step 2: Writing System Tests with Capybara

Capybara allows you to simulate interactions with your app in a readable and easy way:

ruby

```ruby
RSpec.feature "User Signups", type: :feature do
  scenario "user can sign up successfully" do
    visit signup_path
    fill_in "First Name", with: "John"
    fill_in "Last Name", with: "Doe"
    fill_in "Email", with: "john@example.com"
    fill_in "Password", with: "password"
    click_button "Sign Up"
```

```
    expect(page).to    have_text("Welcome,    John
Doe!")
  end
end
```

Capybara also supports asynchronous JavaScript behavior, so you can interact with elements even after they've been dynamically rendered.

18.3 Test-Driven Development (TDD) in Rails

What is Test-Driven Development (TDD)?

Test-Driven Development (TDD) is a software development methodology where you write tests before writing the actual code. The process follows these steps:

1. Write a **failing test**.
2. Write the **minimum code** to make the test pass.
3. **Refactor** the code for clarity and efficiency.
4. **Repeat** the cycle for each feature.

Benefits of TDD in Rails

- Ensures your code meets the requirements from the start.

- Helps avoid regressions by providing a safety net of tests.
- Encourages writing modular, testable code.
- Provides clear documentation for the behavior of the application.

Step 1: Write a Failing Test

Start by writing a test for a feature before implementing it. For example, let's write a test for a method `calculate_discount` in a `Cart` model:

ruby

```
RSpec.describe Cart, type: :model do
  it "calculates the correct discount" do
    cart = Cart.new(total_price: 100)
    expect(cart.calculate_discount).to eq(10)
  end
end
```

This test fails because the method `calculate_discount` doesn't exist yet.

Step 2: Implement Code to Pass the Test

Next, write the code to make the test pass:

ruby

```
class Cart < ApplicationRecord
  def calculate_discount
    total_price * 0.10
  end
end
```

Step 3: Refactor

Once the test is passing, you can refactor the code to improve its quality without changing its behavior.

Step 4: Repeat the Cycle

Continue writing tests for new features, ensuring that each test passes before moving on to the next.

Chapter Summary

Unit, integration, and system tests are essential for ensuring your Rails application works as expected. **RSpec** and **Capybara** provide powerful tools for writing clear, maintainable tests. **Test-Driven Development (TDD)** helps you write clean, reliable code while ensuring your app's features work as expected.

In the next chapter, we'll explore **debugging techniques** in Rails to help you identify and fix issues efficiently.

Next Chapter → Debugging Rails Applications

CHAPTER 19

DEBUGGING AND PERFORMANCE OPTIMIZATION

Introduction

In the development lifecycle, identifying and fixing errors is just as important as writing the initial code. Debugging tools and performance optimization techniques are essential for maintaining the stability and speed of your Rails applications. This chapter will focus on using **debugging tools** to troubleshoot issues, **monitoring application performance**, and **profiling database queries** to optimize slow pages.

By the end of this chapter, you will: Learn how to use **debugging tools** to find and fix errors. Monitor the **performance** of your Rails application to ensure smooth operation. Profile **database queries** and optimize **slow pages** to enhance the user experience.

18.1 Finding and Fixing Errors with Debugging Tools

1. Using byebug for Debugging

byebug is a Ruby gem that allows you to pause the execution of your code at any point and interactively inspect the state of your application. This helps to identify bugs and troubleshoot issues in your code.

Step 1: Install byebug

If it's not already included in your Gemfile (it's included by default in development), add it:

ruby

```
gem 'byebug'
```

Run:

sh

```
bundle install
```

Step 2: Insert Breakpoints

Insert byebug into your code where you want to pause execution and inspect the program state:

ruby

```
class PostsController < ApplicationController
  def show
    @post = Post.find(params[:id])
    byebug  # Execution will stop here, and you
can inspect variables
  end
end
```

When the execution reaches byebug, the application will pause, and you will be dropped into an interactive console. You can inspect variables, step through the code, and modify values in real-time.

Step 3: Interact with the Console

Once the application pauses at the byebug statement, you can type Ruby commands in the console to inspect the application state:

ruby

```
@post  # See the current @post object
params  # Check the value of params
```

Use commands like `next` to move to the next line, `step` to step into method calls, or `continue` to resume the program execution.

Step 4: Removing Breakpoints

Once you've finished debugging, be sure to remove the `byebug` statement from your code to avoid stopping the application in production.

---

2. Using `rails console` for Quick Debugging

The **Rails console** is a powerful tool for debugging because it allows you to interact directly with your application and database. You can test model methods, inspect objects, and query the database.

Step 1: Open the Rails Console

To start the Rails console, run:

```sh

rails console
```

Step 2: Interact with Your Application

Once in the console, you can run any Ruby code. For example, you can interact with your `Post` model:

ruby

```
post = Post.find(1)   # Find a post by ID
post.title            # Inspect the title of the
post
```

You can also make changes directly to the database:

ruby

```
post.update(title:  "New  Title")   # Update a
post's title
```

This is useful for quick, ad-hoc debugging and experimenting with data.

18.2 Monitoring Application Performance

1. Using `rails server` Logs for Performance Monitoring

Rails logs can provide important insights into the performance of your application, including how long each request takes and whether any errors or slow operations are occurring.

To enable detailed logging, set the logging level to `debug` in your `config/environments/development.rb`:

```ruby

config.log_level = :debug
```

You can view the logs directly in the terminal when running the server:

```sh

rails server
```

In the logs, you will see timing information for each request, like:

```less

Completed 200 OK in 42ms (Views: 28.5ms | ActiveRecord: 10.3ms)
```

This gives you an idea of how long each part of the request is taking, and whether database queries or rendering time are contributing to slow performance.

2. Using `NewRelic` or `Scout` for Application Performance Monitoring

For production-level performance monitoring, you can use tools like **NewRelic** or **Scout**. These tools integrate with your Rails application and provide detailed reports on request performance, slow database queries, and error tracking.

Step 1: Install NewRelic

Add NewRelic to your `Gemfile`:

```ruby
gem 'newrelic_rpm'
```

Run:

```sh
bundle install
```

You will also need to sign up for a NewRelic account and configure it with your license key.

Step 2: Configure NewRelic

Once NewRelic is installed, configure it by setting your license key in `config/newrelic.yml`. This will allow NewRelic to monitor your application's performance in production.

Step 3: Monitor Performance

NewRelic provides a web-based dashboard that shows the performance of your application over time, including the slowest requests, database queries, and external API calls. This can help you identify bottlenecks in your application.

18.3 Profiling Database Queries and Optimizing Slow Pages

1. Using `rails db:profiler` for Query Profiling

`rails db:profiler` allows you to profile the database queries your Rails application is executing. This can help identify slow queries or unnecessary database calls.

To enable query profiling, run:

```sh

```

```
rails db:profiler
```

This will output a report showing how long each query took to execute. This helps identify **N+1 queries**, redundant database calls, or long-running queries.

2. Using Bullet Gem for N+1 Query Detection

N+1 queries occur when an application makes additional database queries in a loop that could have been optimized by eager loading. For example, in a loop of posts, querying for each post's associated comments without eager loading the comments causes unnecessary database hits.

Step 1: Install Bullet Gem

Add **Bullet** to your `Gemfile`:

```ruby

```

```
gem 'bullet'
```

Run:

```sh
```

```
bundle install
```

Step 2: Configure Bullet in
config/environments/development.rb

Enable Bullet's N+1 query detection:

```ruby
```

```
config.after_initialize do
  Bullet.enable = true
  Bullet.alert = true
end
```

Bullet will now notify you in the browser if it detects any N+1 queries, helping you optimize your database access.

---

3. Optimizing Slow Pages with Caching

One of the most effective ways to improve page load times for slow pages is by **caching**.

- **Page Caching** stores the entire HTML of a page and serves it without any further processing.

- **Fragment Caching** caches sections of a page that don't change often.
- **Low-Level Caching** stores data (like database query results) to avoid recomputing it.

In Rails, you can implement caching to drastically reduce the time taken to render pages. For example, to cache a page:

ruby

```
caches_page :show
```

To cache fragments:

ruby

```
<%= cache @post do %>
  <%= render @post %>
<% end %>
```

Step 4: Analyze and Optimize Slow Pages

For slow pages, start by checking:

1. **Database queries**: Are there unnecessary or redundant queries? Use eager loading (`includes`) to reduce queries.

2. **Rendering time**: Is the page rendering slow due to complex views? Use partials and caching to speed up rendering.

3. **Assets**: Ensure that JavaScript and CSS are minimized and served via a CDN.

Chapter Summary

Debugging tools like `byebug` and the `rails console` are essential for identifying and fixing errors quickly. **Performance monitoring** tools like `NewRelic` or `Scout` provide valuable insights into how your application is performing in production. **Profiling database queries** using `rails db:profiler` and the **Bullet gem** helps you optimize slow queries and avoid N+1 problems. **Caching strategies** (page, fragment, and low-level caching) can significantly speed up your application by reducing database load and speeding up page rendering.

In the next chapter, we will explore **advanced techniques for scaling Rails applications** and handling high traffic efficiently.

Next Chapter → Scaling Rails Applications

CHAPTER 20

DEPLOYING RAILS APPLICATIONS

Introduction

Deploying a Rails application to production involves configuring the server, setting up your application for production, and automating the deployment process. In this chapter, we will cover how to deploy a Rails application to popular cloud platforms such as **Heroku**, **AWS**, and **DigitalOcean**. We'll also discuss how to set up **CI/CD pipelines** for automating deployment and managing **environment variables** and **secrets** securely.

By the end of this chapter, you will: Understand how to deploy Rails applications to **Heroku**, **AWS**, and **DigitalOcean**. Learn how to set up **CI/CD pipelines** to automate the deployment process. Securely manage **environment variables** and **secrets** in your production environment.

21.1 Deploying to Heroku

1. What is Heroku?

Heroku is a **platform-as-a-service (PaaS)** that allows you to deploy, manage, and scale your applications without worrying about the infrastructure. Heroku abstracts away the underlying server management, making it easy to deploy and scale your Rails applications.

Step 1: Install the Heroku CLI

First, you need to install the **Heroku CLI** on your local machine. You can download it from the Heroku Dev Center.

After installation, log in to Heroku:

sh

```
heroku login
```

Step 2: Prepare Your Rails Application

Ensure your Rails application is ready for production by performing the following tasks:

- Set `config/environments/production.rb` to use the correct database configurations and caching settings.
- Add the **pg gem** for PostgreSQL (Heroku uses PostgreSQL as the default database):

ruby

```
gem 'pg', '>= 0.18', '< 2.0'
```

Run:

sh

```
bundle install
```

- Commit all changes to Git.

Step 3: Create a Heroku App

In your terminal, navigate to your Rails application folder and run:

sh

```
heroku create your-app-name
```

This will create a new Heroku application with the name `your-app-name` (or generate a random name if you don't specify one).

Step 4: Deploy to Heroku

Deploy the application using Git:

sh

```
git push heroku master
```

Heroku will automatically detect your Rails app and install the required dependencies (e.g., Ruby, Rails, PostgreSQL). Once the push is complete, Heroku will trigger a build process, followed by starting the application.

Step 5: Migrate the Database

After deploying, you need to run the database migrations on Heroku:

sh

```
heroku run rake db:migrate
```

Step 6: Open Your Application

You can open your Rails app by running:

sh

```
heroku open
```

Your application should now be live on Heroku!

---

1. What is AWS?

Amazon Web Services (AWS) provides cloud computing services, including infrastructure (EC2), databases (RDS), and storage (S3). AWS gives you complete control over the configuration of your environment, making it suitable for larger, more customized deployments.

Step 1: Set Up an EC2 Instance

To deploy your Rails application on AWS, you need to create an EC2 instance (a virtual server).

- Log in to your AWS Management Console.
- Create a new EC2 instance (choose a lightweight instance like `t2.micro` for testing purposes).
- Select **Ubuntu** as your operating system.
- Configure the security group to allow HTTP, HTTPS, and SSH access.

Step 2: SSH into Your EC2 Instance

Once your EC2 instance is running, you can SSH into it:

sh

```
ssh -i "your-key.pem" ubuntu@your-ec2-public-dns
```

Step 3: Set Up the Environment

Once you're logged into your EC2 instance, install the necessary dependencies to run Rails:

sh

```
sudo apt update
sudo apt install -y curl git libpq-dev postgresql
postgresql-contrib
sudo apt install -y ruby-full
```

Install **Nginx** to serve your application:

sh

```
sudo apt install -y nginx
```

Step 4: Deploy Your Application

1. Clone your Rails app from GitHub to the server:

258

```
sh
```

```
git clone https://github.com/your-user/your-repo.git
```

2. Navigate to your project directory and install the dependencies:

```
sh
```

```
cd your-repo
bundle install
```

3. Set up your **database**:

```
sh
```

```
sudo -u postgres createuser --pwprompt --createdb
--superuser --login --pwprompt your_username
rails db:create db:migrate
```

4. Set up **Nginx** to serve your Rails app (configuration file).

Step 5: Deploy and Access Your Application

Once the app is set up and Nginx is configured, you can access your Rails app using your EC2 instance's public DNS or IP address.

21.3 Deploying to DigitalOcean

1. What is DigitalOcean?

DigitalOcean is another cloud provider that offers simple cloud infrastructure for developers. DigitalOcean provides **Droplets** (virtual servers) and other cloud services, making it an easy-to-use option for deploying Rails applications.

Step 1: Create a Droplet

- Log in to the DigitalOcean Dashboard.
- Create a new Droplet (select Ubuntu as your operating system).
- Set up the firewall and allow SSH and HTTP/HTTPS access.

Step 2: SSH into Your Droplet

After creating your droplet, SSH into the instance:

```sh
ssh root@your-droplet-ip
```

Step 3: Set Up the Environment

Set up the environment by installing the required dependencies:

sh

```
sudo apt update
sudo apt install -y curl git postgresql libpq-
dev nginx
sudo apt install -y ruby-full
```

Install **PostgreSQL**:

sh

```
sudo apt install postgresql postgresql-contrib
```

Step 4: Deploy Your Application

Clone your repository:

sh

```
git clone https://github.com/your-user/your-
repo.git
cd your-repo
```

Install dependencies:

sh

```
bundle install
```

Set up the **database**:

```
sh
```

```
rails db:create db:migrate
```

Step 5: Set Up Nginx and Deploy

You will configure Nginx as your reverse proxy to serve the Rails app and ensure it's running in the background (you can use **systemd** to manage this).

21.4 Setting Up CI/CD Pipelines

1. What is CI/CD?

Continuous Integration (CI) and **Continuous Deployment (CD)** are software development practices that automate the process of testing and deploying code. **CI/CD pipelines** ensure that code changes are automatically tested and deployed, reducing manual errors and speeding up the deployment process.

Step 1: Setting Up GitHub Actions for CI/CD

GitHub Actions allows you to set up a CI/CD pipeline directly in GitHub repositories. Here's how to set it up:

1. Create a `.github/workflows` directory in your repository.
2. Add a `ci.yml` file to define the pipeline configuration:

```yaml
name: Rails CI

on:
  push:
    branches:
      - main
  pull_request:
    branches:
      - main

jobs:
  test:
    runs-on: ubuntu-latest
    services:
      postgres:
        image: postgres:12
        ports:
          - 5432:5432
```

```
env:
    POSTGRES_DB: test
    POSTGRES_USER: user
    POSTGRES_PASSWORD: password
steps:
  - uses: actions/checkout@v2
  - name: Set up Ruby
    uses: ruby/setup-ruby@v1
    with:
      ruby-version: 2.7
  - name: Install dependencies
    run: |
      gem install bundler
      bundle install
  - name: Run tests
    run: |
      bin/rails db:create
      bin/rails db:migrate
      bin/rails test
```

This pipeline will run tests on every push to the `main` branch, using **PostgreSQL** for the database.

21.5 Managing Environment Variables and Secrets

1. Why Manage Secrets?

Sensitive data such as API keys, passwords, and database credentials should never be hardcoded in your application code. Instead, use **environment variables** to store these secrets securely.

Step 1: Using `dotenv` for Development

In development, you can use the **dotenv** gem to load environment variables from a `.env` file.

Add `dotenv` to your Gemfile:

```ruby
gem 'dotenv-rails', groups: [:development, :test]
```

Then run:

```sh
bundle install
```

Create a `.env` file in the root of your project:

```sh
```

```
DATABASE_URL=postgres://user:password@localhost
/db_name
SECRET_KEY_BASE=your-secret-key
```

This file will be loaded automatically in development and test environments.

Step 2: Managing Secrets in Production

In production environments (Heroku, AWS, DigitalOcean), set environment variables directly through the platform:

- **Heroku**: Use `heroku config:set` to set environment variables.
- **AWS**: Use **Elastic Beanstalk** configuration or **AWS Systems Manager**.
- **DigitalOcean**: Use **DO API** to set up environment variables.

Chapter Summary

Heroku, **AWS**, and **DigitalOcean** are great options for deploying Rails applications, each offering different levels of control and ease of use. **CI/CD pipelines** automate testing and deployment, improving the reliability and speed of your development process.

Environment variables and **secrets management** help keep sensitive information secure in production.

In the next chapter, we will explore the **maintenance** of Rails applications, focusing on updates, monitoring, and error tracking.

Next Chapter → Maintenance and Error Tracking in Rails

CHAPTER 21

MONITORING AND LOGGING IN PRODUCTION

Introduction

In production environments, it is critical to monitor your application for performance, errors, and unexpected issues. Effective logging and monitoring not only help identify and resolve issues quickly but also allow you to track user behavior, system performance, and application health over time. In this chapter, we will explore how to set up **logging** with **Lograge** and **Rails logs**, **monitoring** with tools like **New Relic** and **Skylight**, and how to handle **errors** with **Sentry** and **Bugsnag**.

By the end of this chapter, you will: Understand how to set up **efficient logging** for Rails applications using **Lograge**. Learn how to use **New Relic** and **Skylight** to monitor the performance of your Rails application in production. Explore how to handle and track **errors** using **Sentry** and **Bugsnag**.

21.1 Setting Up Logging with Lograge and Rails Logs

1. Why Use Logging in Production?

Logs are essential for monitoring your application's behavior in production. They can provide information about:

- User actions and events.
- System performance, such as request and response times.
- Errors and exceptions that occur in the application.

In Rails, **logs** are generated by default in the `log` directory (`log/development.log`, `log/production.log`), but they can become difficult to read and manage, especially in a production environment.

2. Using Lograge for Better Logging

Lograge is a gem that enhances the default Rails logging by making the logs more concise, structured, and easier to analyze. It reduces the verbosity of Rails logs and provides a cleaner, more consistent log format for production.

Step 1: Install Lograge

Add the **Lograge** gem to your `Gemfile`:

```ruby
gem 'lograge'
```

Then run:

```sh
bundle install
```

Step 2: Configure Lograge

In `config/environments/production.rb`, **enable and** configure Lograge:

```ruby
Rails.application.configure do
  # Use Lograge for production logs
  config.lograge.enabled = true

  # Optional: Customize the log format
  config.lograge.formatter                          =
Lograge::Formatters::Json.new
```

```
# Optional: Add additional custom fields to the
log
  config.lograge.custom_options  =  lambda  do
|event|
    { time: event.time }
  end
end
```

This configuration makes the logs more compact and outputs logs in **JSON format**, which is easier to parse and analyze by external systems (e.g., log aggregation services like **Splunk** or **ELK stack**).

Step 3: Test the Logs

Once Lograge is enabled, Rails will log a single line for each request in production. For example:

json

```
{
  "method":"GET",
  "path":"/posts",
  "status":200,
  "duration":32.5,
  "time":"2022-04-01T12:34:56.789Z"
}
```

271

You can customize the format further to include any additional information (e.g., request headers, user IDs).

1. Why Monitor Your Application?

Application performance monitoring (APM) is critical in production to identify slow requests, database bottlenecks, or external service failures. Tools like **New Relic** and **Skylight** provide real-time insights into the performance of your application, helping you track and resolve performance issues proactively.

2. Monitoring with New Relic

New Relic is a widely used performance monitoring tool that gives you deep insights into your application's performance, including:

- Response times and throughput.
- Error rates and stack traces.
- Slow database queries.
- External service calls (e.g., API requests).

Step 1: Install the New Relic Gem

Add the **newrelic_rpm** gem to your `Gemfile`:

```ruby
```

```
gem 'newrelic_rpm'
```

Run:

```sh
```

```
bundle install
```

Step 2: Configure New Relic

After installing the gem, you will need to configure New Relic by adding your license key to the `config/newrelic.yml` file. You can find your license key in the **New Relic dashboard** under Account settings.

In the `newrelic.yml` file, set the environment to production and enter your license key:

```yaml
```

```
common: &default_settings
  license_key: 'YOUR_NEW_RELIC_LICENSE_KEY'
  app_name: 'Your Rails Application'
```

Step 3: View Application Metrics

Once New Relic is configured, it will automatically start monitoring your app. You can log into the New Relic dashboard and view metrics such as:

- **Web transaction times**: How long it takes to process HTTP requests.
- **Database query performance**: How long database queries are taking.
- **External service performance**: The time spent on API requests or third-party services.

New Relic's dashboard will give you valuable insights into which parts of your application need optimization.

3. Monitoring with Skylight

Skylight is another performance monitoring tool designed specifically for **Rails applications**. It provides insights into how your app is performing by measuring **request times**, **database queries**, and **overall performance**.

Step 1: Install the Skylight Gem

Add the **skylight** gem to your `Gemfile`:

```ruby
ruby
```

```ruby
gem 'skylight'
```

Run:

```sh
sh
```

```sh
bundle install
```

Step 2: Configure Skylight

Once the gem is installed, sign up for an account at Skylight.io and get your **Skylight API key**. Then configure Skylight in your `config/initializers/skylight.rb`:

```ruby
ruby
```

```ruby
Skylight.configure do |config|
  config.authentication = 'YOUR_API_KEY'
end
```

Step 3: View Skylight Metrics

After configuring Skylight, it will automatically start monitoring the performance of your Rails application. You can view detailed metrics in the Skylight dashboard, such as:

- **Request durations**.
- **Slow database queries**.
- **Slowest actions**.

Skylight also provides insights into performance bottlenecks by showing which parts of your code are taking the most time.

21.3 Handling Errors with Sentry and Bugsnag

1. Why Handle Errors?

Error tracking is essential in production to catch exceptions and bugs that users encounter but may not report. Tools like **Sentry** and **Bugsnag** provide real-time error reporting and logging, helping you catch and fix issues before they impact a large number of users.

2. Handling Errors with Sentry

Sentry is an error tracking tool that allows you to capture, monitor, and fix exceptions in real time.

Step 1: Install the Sentry Gem

Add the **sentry-raven** gem to your `Gemfile`:

```ruby
ruby
```

```ruby
gem 'sentry-rails'
```

Run:

```sh
sh
```

```sh
bundle install
```

Step 2: Configure Sentry

Once the gem is installed, configure Sentry with your **DSN** (Data Source Name) from the Sentry dashboard. In `config/initializers/sentry.rb`:

```ruby
ruby
```

```ruby
Sentry.init do |config|
  config.dsn = 'YOUR_SENTRY_DSN'
end
```

277

Step 3: View Errors in Sentry Dashboard

After setting up Sentry, it will automatically capture exceptions that occur in your Rails application and send them to the Sentry dashboard. You can view detailed information about the error, including stack traces, affected users, and request parameters.

---

3. Handling Errors with Bugsnag

Bugsnag is another popular error monitoring tool that captures application errors and provides detailed error reports, including diagnostic data.

Step 1: Install the Bugsnag Gem

Add the **bugsnag** gem to your `Gemfile`:

```ruby

gem 'bugsnag'
```

Run:

```sh
```

```
bundle install
```

Step 2: Configure Bugsnag

Once the gem is installed, configure Bugsnag with your **API key**. In `config/initializers/bugsnag.rb`:

```
ruby
```

```
Bugsnag.configure do |config|
  config.api_key = "YOUR_BUGSNAG_API_KEY"
end
```

Step 3: View Errors in Bugsnag Dashboard

Bugsnag will automatically capture errors that occur in your Rails application and send them to the Bugsnag dashboard. In the dashboard, you can view detailed error reports, including stack traces, the context of the error, and the number of affected users.

Chapter Summary

Lograge enhances the default Rails logging, providing cleaner, more structured logs that are easier to analyze in production.

New Relic and **Skylight** are powerful tools for

performance monitoring, providing insights into request times, database queries, and overall app health. **Sentry** and **Bugsnag** allow you to track and manage **errors** in real-time, helping you fix issues before they affect more users.

In the next chapter, we will explore **maintenance and updates** for Rails applications to ensure long-term stability and scalability.

Next Chapter → Maintenance and Updates in Rails

CHAPTER 22

MAINTAINING AND UPDATING RAILS APPLICATIONS

Introduction

Maintaining and updating Rails applications is crucial to keeping them secure, performant, and up-to-date with the latest features and best practices. As your application grows, you'll need to regularly update **Rails**, manage **dependencies**, and handle **database migrations** safely to ensure the stability of your application. This chapter will guide you through these processes and best practices.

By the end of this chapter, you will:
Understand how to **upgrade Rails** and manage dependencies effectively.
Learn best practices for **keeping gems and libraries updated**.
Gain knowledge on how to **manage database migrations safely** to prevent data loss and downtime.

21.1 Upgrading Rails and Managing Dependencies

1. Upgrading Rails

Rails is continuously improved, and new versions include bug fixes, security patches, performance improvements, and new features. It's important to upgrade Rails regularly to take advantage of these updates. However, upgrading Rails can sometimes be challenging, especially for large applications with many dependencies.

Step 1: Check the Current Version

Before upgrading, check which version of Rails you're currently using:

```sh

rails -v
```

Step 2: Review the Release Notes

Before performing an upgrade, always read the Rails release notes for the version you want to upgrade to. This will highlight breaking changes, new features, deprecations, and necessary actions.

Step 3: Update the Rails Version

To upgrade Rails, modify the version number in your Gemfile:

ruby

```
gem 'rails', '~> 6.1.0'
```

Then run:

sh

```
bundle update rails
```

This command updates the Rails gem and also updates its dependencies in your Gemfile.lock.

Step 4: Update Other Dependencies

After upgrading Rails, some of your other gems might need to be updated to work with the new version. Use:

sh

```
bundle outdated
```

This will show you a list of outdated gems. Update the ones that are compatible with your new Rails version:

sh

```
bundle update <gem_name>
```

Step 5: Run Tests and Check for Deprecations

After upgrading, run your tests to ensure everything works as expected:

sh

```
rails test
```

Also, check for deprecations or warnings related to the upgrade. Rails includes a deprecation warning system that helps identify deprecated features.

sh

```
rails deprecate
```

---

2. Managing Dependencies

Managing dependencies is an essential part of maintaining a Rails application. It's important to keep your dependencies updated to ensure compatibility, security, and performance.

Step 1: Use Bundler for Dependency Management

Bundler helps you manage your application's gems and their versions. To update your gems, use:

sh

```
bundle update
```

This updates all gems to the latest versions allowed by your `Gemfile`.

Step 2: Pin Gem Versions in `Gemfile`

To avoid unexpected issues with gems, it's a good idea to pin the versions of your dependencies. In the `Gemfile`, specify version constraints:

ruby

```
gem 'rails', '~> 6.1.0'
gem 'devise', '~> 4.7'
```

This ensures that you're using a version that is compatible with your application.

Step 3: Review Gem Vulnerabilities

Use the **bundler-audit** gem to check for known security vulnerabilities in your dependencies:

sh

```
gem install bundler-audit
bundler-audit check
```

This helps you identify vulnerabilities in gems that may need immediate updates or replacement.

21.2 Keeping Gems and Libraries Updated

1. Why Keep Gems Updated?

Gem updates often contain important security patches, bug fixes, and performance improvements. Keeping your gems up-to-date ensures your application is running on the latest stable versions and minimizes potential security risks.

Step 1: Update Specific Gems

To update a specific gem, use:

```sh
```

```sh
bundle update <gem_name>
```

For example, to update the `devise` gem, you would run:

```sh
```

```sh
bundle update devise
```

This ensures that only that gem and its dependencies are updated without affecting others.

Step 2: Automate Updates with Dependabot

Dependabot is a GitHub service that automatically creates pull requests to update your dependencies. Enable it by adding the following configuration to your repository in `.github/dependabot.yml`:

```yaml
```

```yaml
version: 2
updates:
  - package-ecosystem: "bundler"
    directory: "/"
    schedule:
      interval: "weekly"
```

Dependabot will create pull requests to keep your gems up-to-date automatically.

Step 3: Test After Updating Gems

After updating your gems, run your test suite to verify that everything works as expected:

```sh

rails test
```

It's essential to ensure that the updates haven't introduced any breaking changes.

21.3 Managing Database Migrations Safely

1. Why Are Database Migrations Important?

Database migrations in Rails allow you to version control your database schema, making it easy to apply schema changes across different environments. However, migrations can be dangerous if not managed properly, as they can lead to data loss or application downtime.

Step 1: Write Safe Migrations

Always ensure that your migrations are **safe**. For example, if you're adding an index or removing a column, do it in a way that avoids locking the table for a long time, especially in production environments.

Example of a Safe Index Creation

ruby

```
class              AddIndexToPosts            <
ActiveRecord::Migration[6.0]
  def change
    add_index    :posts,    :title,    algorithm:
:concurrently
  end
end
```

Using `algorithm:  :concurrently` ensures that the index is added without locking the table.

Example of a Safe Column Removal

ruby

```
class         RemoveOldColumnFromPosts           <
ActiveRecord::Migration[6.0]
  def change
    remove_column     :posts,        :old_column,
if_exists: true
  end
```

```
end
```

The if_exists: true ensures that the migration doesn't fail if the column doesn't exist.

Step 2: Run Migrations in Staging First

Before applying migrations to production, run them in a staging environment first to catch any potential issues. Always test the migration process with real data to ensure it doesn't break your application.

Step 3: Use db:rollback to Undo Migrations

If something goes wrong during a migration, you can roll it back using:

```sh
rails db:rollback
```

This will undo the last migration. You can also rollback multiple migrations with:

```sh
rails db:rollback STEP=3
```

Step 4: Avoid Running Migrations in High-Traffic Times

If you need to run a migration in production, avoid running it during peak traffic times. Instead, schedule migrations during off-peak hours to reduce the risk of downtime or performance degradation.

---

4. Database Backups Before Migrations

Always create a **backup** of your database before running any migrations, especially in production. This ensures that you can quickly restore the database in case of failure.

You can use tools like **pg_dump** for PostgreSQL to create backups:

sh

```
pg_dump -U your_user your_database > backup.sql
```

This allows you to restore the database using the backup in case anything goes wrong.

Chapter Summary

Upgrading Rails and managing dependencies is vital to keep your application secure, performant, and compatible with the latest Rails features. **Keeping gems up-to-date** ensures that you're using the latest stable versions with bug fixes and security patches. **Database migrations** should be handled with care, especially in production environments, to avoid data loss and application downtime.

In the next chapter, we will explore how to scale your Rails application to handle more users and traffic efficiently.

Next Chapter → Scaling Rails Applications

CHAPTER 23

BUILDING A FULL-STACK RAILS APPLICATION

Introduction

Building a full-stack Rails application involves planning the project architecture, implementing features like authentication, CRUD (Create, Read, Update, Delete) operations, and integrating third-party APIs. Once the application is developed, it is essential to deploy the final product to a production environment. In this chapter, we will go step-by-step through the process of building a full-stack Rails application, covering everything from project planning to deployment.

By the end of this chapter, you will:
Understand how to plan and structure a **full-stack Rails application**.
Learn how to implement **authentication**, **CRUD operations**, and **API integrations**.
Gain knowledge of how to **deploy** the final product to a production environment.

24.1 Project Planning and Architecture

1. Defining the Project

Before writing any code, it's essential to plan the project's structure and define the features and requirements. For this example, let's build a **task management** application where users can register, log in, create, update, delete, and list their tasks.

Key Features

- **Authentication**: Users should be able to register, log in, and log out.
- **CRUD Operations**: Users should be able to create, view, update, and delete tasks.
- **API Integrations**: The application will integrate with an external **weather API** to allow users to set weather-related reminders for tasks.

Database Schema

For this project, we'll need at least two models:

- **User** (for authentication)
- **Task** (for managing tasks)

2. Project Architecture

The application will follow the standard **Rails architecture**:

- **MVC (Model-View-Controller)** pattern will handle the core functionality.
- **Database**: We'll use PostgreSQL for managing application data.
- **Authentication**: We'll use **Devise** for handling user authentication.
- **API Integration**: We'll integrate with a weather API to fetch weather data based on the user's location.

24.2 Implementing Authentication, CRUD, and API Integrations

1. Setting Up the Rails Application

Start by creating the new Rails application:

sh

```
rails new task_manager --database=postgresql
cd task_manager
```

Then, set up your **PostgreSQL database**:

```
sh
```

```
rails db:create
```

2. Installing and Setting Up Authentication with Devise

Devise is a popular gem for handling authentication in Rails applications. Let's set it up.

Step 1: Install Devise

Add Devise to your Gemfile:

```ruby
```

```
gem 'devise'
```

Run:

```
sh
```

```
bundle install
rails generate devise:install
```

This will install Devise and create configuration files. Next, generate the User model:

```
sh
```

```
rails generate devise User
rails db:migrate
```

Now, the **User** model will have all the default authentication features such as **sign up**, **login**, and **password management**.

Step 2: Add Authentication to the Application

You can use Devise's helper methods in your controllers and views. In the `application_controller.rb`, add:

```ruby
```

```
before_action :authenticate_user!
```

This will ensure that all pages require authentication except for the pages you explicitly specify.

Step 3: Create Views for Authentication

Devise provides ready-made views for registration and login. You can generate the views and customize them as needed:

```sh
```

```
rails generate devise:views
```

This will create the views in `app/views/devise/` where you can edit them to match your design.

---

3. Implementing CRUD Operations for Tasks

Now, let's create the **Task** model and implement the basic CRUD operations.

Step 1: Generate the Task Model

sh

```
rails generate model Task title:string
description:text user:references
rails db:migrate
```

This will create a `Task` model with `title`, `description`, and `user_id` (as a foreign key to associate each task with a user).

Step 2: Set Up Associations

In `app/models/user.rb`, establish the association between users and tasks:

```
ruby
```

```ruby
class User < ApplicationRecord
  has_many :tasks, dependent: :destroy
  # Devise modules here
end
```

In `app/models/task.rb`, set the inverse association:

```
ruby
```

```ruby
class Task < ApplicationRecord
  belongs_to :user
  validates :title, presence: true
end
```

Step 3: Create the Tasks Controller

Generate a controller for managing tasks:

```
sh
```

```
rails generate controller Tasks
```

In `app/controllers/tasks_controller.rb`, implement the basic CRUD actions:

```
ruby
```

```ruby
class TasksController < ApplicationController
```

```
  before_action :set_task, only: [:show, :edit,
:update, :destroy]

  def index
    @tasks = current_user.tasks
  end

  def show
  end

  def new
    @task = current_user.tasks.build
  end

  def create
    @task                                      =
current_user.tasks.build(task_params)
    if @task.save
      redirect_to  @task,  notice:  'Task  was
successfully created.'
    else
      render :new
    end
  end

  def edit
  end

  def update
```

```
    if @task.update(task_params)
      redirect_to    @task,    notice:    'Task    was
successfully updated.'
    else
      render :edit
    end
  end

  def destroy
    @task.destroy
    redirect_to   tasks_url,   notice:   'Task   was
successfully destroyed.'
  end

  private

  def set_task
    @task = current_user.tasks.find(params[:id])
  end

  def task_params
    params.require(:task).permit(:title,
:description)
  end
end
```

Step 4: Create Views for Tasks

Create views for displaying tasks. In `app/views/tasks/`,
create the necessary views (`index.html.erb`,

`show.html.erb, new.html.erb, edit.html.erb`) for the CRUD actions.

---

4. Implementing API Integration

Now, let's integrate an external weather API to fetch weather-related reminders for tasks. We'll use the **OpenWeatherMap API** as an example.

Step 1: Sign Up for the API

Sign up at OpenWeatherMap and obtain your API key.

Step 2: Install HTTParty Gem for API Requests

Add the **HTTParty** gem to your `Gemfile`:

```ruby
gem 'httparty'
```

Run:

```sh
bundle install
```

Step 3: Fetch Weather Data

Create a service to interact with the weather API. For example, in `app/services/weather_service.rb`:

ruby

```
class WeatherService
  include HTTParty
  base_uri
'https://api.openweathermap.org/data/2.5/weathe
r'

  def initialize(city)
    @city = city
    @api_key = 'YOUR_API_KEY'
  end

  def fetch_weather
    self.class.get('', query: { q: @city, appid:
@api_key })
  end
end
```

Step 4: Use Weather Data in Tasks

In your `TasksController`, you can call the weather service when creating a task:

ruby

```
class TasksController < ApplicationController
  def create
    @task                          =
current_user.tasks.build(task_params)
    weather        =        WeatherService.new('New
York').fetch_weather
    if @task.save
      # You can save weather-related info to the
task or display it to the user
      @task.update(weather_info:
weather['weather'][0]['description'])
      redirect_to  @task,  notice:  'Task  was
successfully created.'
    else
      render :new
    end
  end
end
```

24.3 Deploying the Final Product

1. Preparing for Deployment

Before deploying your Rails application, ensure the
following:

- Set up environment variables (e.g., for API keys, Rails secrets).
- Configure the production database and other services (e.g., Redis, Amazon S3 for file storage).
- Ensure all assets are precompiled for production.

Run:

sh

```
RAILS_ENV=production rails assets:precompile
```

2. Deploying to Heroku

For simplicity, we'll deploy the application to **Heroku**.

Step 1: Create a Heroku App
sh

```
heroku create task-manager
```
Step 2: Set Environment Variables
sh

```
heroku                              config:set
OPENWEATHERMAP_API_KEY=your_api_key
```
Step 3: Push to Heroku
sh

```
git push heroku master
```

Step 4: Migrate the Database on Heroku

```
sh
```

```
heroku run rake db:migrate
```

Step 5: Open the Application

```
sh
```

```
heroku open
```

Your application should now be live on Heroku!

Chapter Summary

Project planning and architecture are critical steps in building a full-stack Rails application. **Authentication** can be easily handled using **Devise**, while **CRUD operations** can be implemented for managing resources like tasks.

API integrations can be implemented to enhance your app with external data, such as weather information for task reminders.

The final product can be deployed to platforms like **Heroku**, ensuring easy scalability and management.

In the next chapter, we will explore **advanced topics in Rails**, such as background job processing, advanced caching, and more.

Next Chapter → Advanced Rails Techniques

CHAPTER 24

BEST PRACTICES AND FUTURE
OF RAILS

Introduction

Ruby on Rails has been a popular framework for web development for many years, providing a powerful and efficient way to build web applications. However, as with any technology, maintaining high-quality code, staying up to date with framework updates, and anticipating future trends is essential to keep your application robust, scalable, and secure. In this chapter, we will discuss **best practices** for code organization and maintainability, how to **keep up with Rails updates**, and the **future of Ruby on Rails** in the world of web development.

By the end of this chapter, you will: Understand **best practices** for **code organization** and **maintainability** in Rails applications. Learn how to **keep up with Rails updates** to ensure your application remains secure and up to date. Explore the **future of Ruby on Rails** and how it continues to evolve in the web development ecosystem.

24.1 Code Organization and Maintainability

1. Why Code Organization and Maintainability Matter

Good code organization makes your application easier to understand, extend, and maintain. As your application grows, it's important to adopt patterns and practices that keep your codebase clean, modular, and easy to manage. Without good organization, your application could become difficult to debug, extend, or scale.

2. Folder Structure Best Practices

Rails provides a convention-over-configuration approach, and following these conventions is a key practice for maintainability. Below are some guidelines for maintaining a clean folder structure:

1. Models

Models should focus on business logic and data manipulation. If a model is becoming too large or complex, consider moving the logic into **service objects** or **concerns**.

For example, if a `User` model has too many responsibilities, you could extract payment processing into a `PaymentService`.

ruby

```
class PaymentService
  def initialize(user)
    @user = user
  end

  def charge(amount)
    # handle payment logic here
  end
end
```

2. Controllers

Controllers should be lightweight and focused on coordinating between models and views. Controllers should delegate business logic to models or service objects, rather than contain complex logic themselves.

If your controllers grow large, consider using **concerns** or **decorators** to extract logic.

ruby

```
class PostsController < ApplicationController
```

```ruby
  include PostFilter

  def index
    @posts = filtered_posts
  end
end
```

3. Views

Keep views as simple as possible by limiting the amount of logic in them. Use partials for reusable components. Avoid placing complex logic in views—if needed, move it to helper methods or presenters.

ruby

```
# app/views/posts/_post.html.erb
<%= render partial: "posts/post", locals: { post: @post } %>
```

4. Services and Concerns

For complex logic that doesn't belong in models or controllers, consider creating **services** or **concerns**. Service objects encapsulate business logic that can be reused across different parts of the application.

ruby

```
class OrderService
```

```
def initialize(order)
  @order = order
end

def process
  # business logic for processing orders
end
end
```

Concerns are great for sharing functionality between models or controllers.

```
ruby
```

```
# app/models/concerns/taggable.rb
module Taggable
  extend ActiveSupport::Concern

  included do
    has_many :tags
  end
end
```

3. Testing and Test-Driven Development (TDD)

To keep your application maintainable, adopt a comprehensive testing strategy. **RSpec** and **Capybara** are popular testing libraries in Rails that help ensure that your application's functionality remains intact as you make changes.

- Write **unit tests** for models.
- Use **integration tests** to test interactions between controllers and models.
- Implement **system tests** using Capybara for end-to-end testing.

Test-driven development (TDD) can help you design your code better while ensuring it remains flexible and bug-free over time.

24.2 Keeping Up with Rails Updates

1. Why Keep Up with Rails Updates?

Rails is constantly evolving with new features, bug fixes, performance improvements, and security patches. Keeping your application up-to-date is crucial for:

- **Security**: New releases often include security patches to fix vulnerabilities.
- **Performance**: Rails updates may include optimizations that improve your app's speed and scalability.

- **New Features**: Rails introduces new features that can simplify your codebase and improve the user experience.
- **Deprecation Warnings**: Rails deprecates old functionality over time, and keeping your app up-to-date ensures you don't rely on outdated or unsupported features.

2. Upgrading Rails

To upgrade Rails, follow these best practices:

- **Check the release notes**: Before upgrading, always review the release notes to understand the breaking changes and new features.
- **Upgrade in stages**: If you're upgrading across multiple versions (e.g., from 5.2 to 6.1), consider upgrading one version at a time to avoid larger conflicts.
- **Run tests after upgrading**: Ensure your test suite passes after upgrading Rails to make sure your app still functions correctly.
- **Use the `rails app:update` command**: This command updates configuration files and assets when upgrading Rails.

Example Upgrade Process:

1. Update the Rails version in `Gemfile`:

```
ruby
```

```
gem 'rails', '~> 6.1.0'
```

2. Run:

```sh
```

```
bundle update rails
```

3. Run migrations:

```sh
```

```
rails db:migrate
```

4. Check deprecation warnings:

```sh
```

```
rails deprecate
```

5. Run tests and manually check the application for issues.

3. Handling Gems and Dependencies

When upgrading Rails, you'll also need to manage your gem dependencies. Use tools like **Bundler** and **Dependabot** to keep your gems up-to-date and avoid outdated versions that may break your application.

- **Bundler**: Run `bundle update` to update all gems to their latest versions.
- **Dependabot**: Enable Dependabot to automatically create pull requests to update gems.
- **Check compatibility**: Make sure your gems are compatible with the version of Rails you're upgrading to. This might require updating some gems to newer versions.

24.3 The Future of Ruby on Rails in Web Development

1. Continued Focus on Developer Happiness

Ruby on Rails has always been focused on **developer productivity**, and this will continue to be a guiding principle. Rails developers benefit from a large community, extensive documentation, and a rich ecosystem of gems that make building web applications fast and easy. Expect the framework to continue evolving with a focus on:

- **Simplicity**: Rails will continue to make it easier to build applications with fewer lines of code.

- **Convention over configuration**: The Rails philosophy will continue to provide sensible defaults and built-in conventions that help developers avoid unnecessary decisions.

2. Hotwire and the Future of Frontend Development

The future of Rails frontend development is heavily tied to **Hotwire**, a set of technologies introduced by Basecamp that emphasizes building modern applications with minimal JavaScript. Hotwire consists of:

- **Turbo**: Enables fast page updates without requiring a full page reload by using HTML over the wire.
- **Stimulus**: Adds lightweight JavaScript to HTML for interactivity without the complexity of large frontend frameworks like React or Vue.js.

This approach streamlines development by using more server-side rendering and reducing reliance on JavaScript-heavy frontends, making it a compelling alternative to the traditional single-page application (SPA) model.

3. WebSockets and Real-Time Applications

With the rise of real-time applications (e.g., chat apps, live notifications), Rails will likely continue to improve its WebSocket capabilities through **ActionCable**. Rails already offers great support for WebSockets, but expect further improvements to make building real-time features even easier and more efficient.

4. Multi-Platform Support and API-First Applications

As the demand for APIs grows (especially with mobile apps and third-party integrations), Rails will likely continue enhancing its support for **API-only applications**. Expect improvements in building fast, secure APIs that can easily integrate with various platforms and services.

Additionally, **multi-platform development** is gaining traction. Rails will continue to support **cross-platform development**, including integration with mobile applications (via **React Native** or **Flutter**) and serverless technologies.

Chapter Summary

Code organization and maintainability are crucial for building scalable and manageable Rails applications. Use service objects, concerns, and testing to keep your codebase clean.

Keeping up with Rails updates is essential for staying secure, improving performance, and taking advantage of new features. Use tools like **Bundler** and **Dependabot** to manage dependencies effectively.

The **future of Ruby on Rails** involves a continued focus on **developer happiness**, improved support for **real-time features**, **Hotwire** for frontend development, and a growing emphasis on **API-first** applications.

In the next chapter, we'll explore how to **scale** your Rails applications and handle high-traffic scenarios efficiently.

Next Chapter → Scaling Rails Applications